BRAVE ENOUGH NOW

BRAVE ENOUGH NOW

An inspirational story of self-discovery, survival and hope

TIFFANY JOHNSON

INDEPENDENT INK

INDEPENDENT

First published 2019 by Independent Ink
PO Box 1638, Carindale
Queensland 4152 Australia
independentink.com.au

Copyright © Tiffany Johnson 2019

ISBN 978-0-6485879-0-3 (paperback)
ISBN 978-0-6485879-1-0 (epub)
ISBN 978-0-6485879-2-7 (kindle)

 A catalogue record for this
book is available from the
National Library of Australia

Typeset in Garamond 12/17 pt by Post Pre-press Group
Cover Design: Maria Biaggini @ Independent Ink
Cover image: depositphotos©rfphoto

For Jan, Carolynn, Briana, Jim and Kylie

CONTENTS

AUTHOR'S NOTE

This is my story – not mine alone, but mine.

I have worked closely with a small group of individuals who have helped me write this book. I have called upon my own journals, photographs and memories of my life during the time this book is set. I have researched and investigated some of the events where appropriate.

I have changed the names of most, but not all, individuals in this book. 'Cassandra' really is Cassandra; she remains my best friend to this day.

This story is about finding myself and is based on my own life events. I have omitted some people and events, as they had no impact on the story I am telling. Certain scenes have been altered for privacy reasons.

Some scenes within this book might trigger emotions in victims of trauma. If you need to talk to someone about your situation, contact SANE on 1800 187 263 or via their website www.sane.org, alternatively contact Lifeline on 13 11 14 or via their website www.lifeline.org.au.

So, with all the puzzle pieces of myself now found, here is my story.

PROLOGUE

Thunderous water gushed all around me. I had surrendered my body as I was swept away by the ravaging floodwaters, and I was now submerged in thick mud, caught up in the swirling torrent. The only noise I could hear was the pounding of the water as it crushed my body, twisting and turning as if I was in a washing machine. My aching lungs clung to what precious air I had left in them and then . . . a moment . . . a push . . . a shove as my back was pushed up against a hard, cold boulder by the force of a giant log, and then my head broke through the surface and my depleted lungs finally filled with air.

For the first time, I saw what I was in.

I had been engulfed by a deluge of water so wild, so ferocious, it looked like a giant chocolate milkshake still in the blender as it pounded its way down the Saxetenbach Gorge in Switzerland.

Another giant log rammed into my stomach as rapids ran wild over my body. Its force was like that of a car slamming on its brakes, and it pushed my back further up the boulder, crushing me. I could hear the deluge raging down the mountainside, the sound hammering in my ears, yet all I could feel was the air – the exquisite, pure, delightful air replenishing my lungs – air to breathe in and air to breathe out.

I looked to my right as I tried to orientate myself, and I saw the lifeless bodies of my friends, face down, floating past me on top of the torrent.

I looked straight ahead, back up the mountain, to where I had been standing just moments before, among friends abuzz with anticipation of the adventures that lay ahead. Had it been minutes, or seconds ago? I was no longer sure.

The clear waters of moments before had now turned into an unrestrained effusion of mud-filled water. Copious amounts of debris were strangling us all – sticks, twigs, rocks, logs and boulders, all moving in chaotic rhythm with the water. Giant waves rose up seemingly from nowhere within the water flowing violently down the mountainside.

I looked to my left and saw a bank shrouded in natural green beauty: soft, green leaves vibrated against the wild wind; moss covered every corner. It was not too far away, but far enough that safety there was out of reach.

I would never make it.

At that moment, with the clean, crisp mountain air finally filling my lungs, I was trapped in the Saxetenbach Gorge in the majestic Swiss Alps. The clouds encircling their peaks had unleashed this hell on us.

In that one nanosecond, I could see my whole life – where I had come from, what I had been through. But where was I headed? Did I have any control over where I went next?

My whole childhood had been so different from the life I was now living, as a 21-year-old woman filled with wanderlust and a thirst for adventure.

I had come from a happy childhood, a loving middle-class Australian family, with devoted parents – my true place of belonging, my only place of belonging. My mother – my best friend, my confidant, and my safety net – someone I could always turn to, no matter what I was going through or where I was headed. My father, who nurtured me and adored me, showed me how to have strength and courage. My little brother looked up to me, followed me.

I was trusting of everyone, always looking to do the right thing – I was the quintessential 'girl next door'. Petite, with delicate pale skin, long blonde curly hair and blue eye – 'Bright Eyes', my teachers had called me in our little country town, where everyone knew me, and I knew them.

The thing was, I never felt like I was whole, that I was 'me'. Something was missing.

That feeling of being less than complete, of never honestly feeling whole, of not belonging had brought me to this place and time, trying to work it all out. I had stumbled, fallen, got lost and backtracked numerous times on my journey to this point, and now I was travelling through Europe, still desperately trying to find my missing piece, wanting to be whole, trying to find who I truly was.

In the middle of this torrent of destruction, with water hellishly lapping at my chin and mud covering my limbs, cramming underneath my fingernails and into my ears, coating my eyelids and eyelashes, and sliding up my nose as it pushed past me, I finally had found myself. Not at that exact moment, but only hours before, when my travel companions and I were connected in a way that travelling together can bring. There was acceptance of each other, of who we each were, with no judgments, no control, no expectations. A special bond tied us together, and I didn't want to let go. This new community of people who despite our different histories, different lives and different experiences, offered no judgement of each other, just love and an acknowledgement of how curious life can be. A community that accepted me – all of me.

And now they were dead.

The turbulent slurry filled with branches and large logs was rising higher by the second, whipping every inch of my body, swirling violently and blasting lightning bolts of pain through my skin as each log collided with me on its way down the mountainside. There was no stopping it.

Pinned under the weight of the watery fury, my back pressed hard against the boulder, I couldn't turn to see where the torrent of water went as it raged down the canyon, and where it would take me.

I saw my life playing out like a series of snapshots. Unable to scramble to the top of the boulder behind me, but momentarily spared from the coursing water by the log in front of me, I pondered how long I could wait for someone to possibly come and rescue me. Would anyone even come? Or would my hesitation just end up with my being subsumed by the rising waters or crushed by another log?

Or should I take charge of my own destiny?

Do I stay here or do I let go?

As much as exhaustion was starting to overwhelm my surging adrenalin, I was more tired of waiting for others to determine my fate. And with that thought and the thought of what had led me to this place, unable to see what was ahead of me, I let go.

Chapter 1

CAN I EVER BE FOUND?

Sitting on the hillside on our family farm, in rural New South Wales, Australia, I was back home. Surrounded by rabbit holes, willy wag tails twitching their feathers and singing their sweet song, I watched on as wombats meandered slowly through the grass. I was back in my safe space, after years of being away.

Though I loved my home on the farm, I'd never felt comfortable in my small home town, where everyone knew everyone, and everything about you. It had always felt confining. I couldn't sneeze without someone saying, 'Bless you'. I'd never felt like I belonged in our tiny country town. I had always wished for a place to truly belong, a place where I could be the real me. It had only been when I went to high school that I had started to settle into my own skin, removing myself from the claustrophobia of our town, but still, I hadn't felt like I'd belonged.

Even back then, I had been ready for a new life, filled with adventure, new experiences. I was thirsty for something more, though I wasn't initially sure what that 'more' was.

After high school, I had thought I would find it when I moved onto the next chapter of my life at university, but it had been more of the same small-town ways I had been so desperate to leave.

After university, I had moved to the city. Living in the city was nothing like my upbringing in the country. The city was something else, and it was what I had been craving. I got a job as a waitress in a funky new café and I was desperate to make a good impression. I felt perplexed by all the knobs and buttons on the coffee machine, the yelling from the kitchen, the hustle and bustle of a busy street – it was all so foreign to me. I couldn't understand why for someone who was a good cook, this coffee-making business was so tricky!

It was while I was flustered trying to get the hang of my new gig that I saw him, the cute Englishman wanting his morning coffee.

I'd seen him around. He was charming, witty and with an accent that made me melt. He was tall with blond hair, and eyes, oh those eyes . . . they were a deeper blue than the darkest blue of the ocean, almost black. I felt tingles up and down my spine. His smile was wide and his smell divine. Senses stirred in me that I didn't even know existed. Butterflies cavorted in my stomach. The chemistry between us was intense. I felt almost paralysed as sweat poured out of me while I feverishly tried to work the damn coffee machine, but the harder I tried the more I screwed it up, and the more he laughed at me. And the more he laughed the more my heart skipped a beat. Only beating to the drum of Patrick.

But something inside me kept warning me. Stop! Do not go any further! It was my intuition calling me and I should have listened. I knew I should have run a mile, but, he was oh so alluring.

Soon we were inseparable and in the beginning, I thought I had found my missing puzzle piece. I thought my 'something more', that thing I had always been missing, was love and adoration from a partner. I felt a sense of belonging with Patrick. He was older, wilder, the life of the party and I was infatuated with him. I thought I had started to live a real life, the one I had been dreaming of. With the thrill of a new love, exciting and intoxicating, it felt like my life had truly started. But our relationship had an undercurrent of darkness. As I fell head over heels in love, all the pieces of me seemed to vanish, subsumed by the relationship.

And then, the earth began to crumble beneath our feet. The relationship changed direction causing hurt and pain. Once a shimmering pearl filled with love, it soon began to lose its luster and eventually, decayed into a toxic, heated mess. We knew we loved each other, but it was an unhealthy love. During my relationship with Patrick, I lost sight of myself.

I was plagued by doubt and misery, struggling to find the strength to leave what I knew was a harmful relationship. I couldn't understand where I had gone wrong. Why had my life turned in a direction I never saw coming? What was it that I was truly looking for? Would I ever find me? What was I supposed to do? Where was I supposed to be? Where would my life end up?

During this time with Patrick, childhood flashbacks would often come to me. Long-forgotten memories of junior school and the intense bullying resurfaced in my mind at times when my spirit was crushed. The feelings of isolation made me feel just like the little girl I once was: sitting alone on the bench in the playground, with classmates ignoring me or calling out hurtful names, never feeling accepted, never feeling like I belonged. I had turned my back on that person in my teen years, but now as a woman in a relationship filled with turmoil, it had enveloped me once more.

It wasn't until the tragic passing of my beloved Aunty Di that I realised I needed to make some changes to become the woman she knew I could be.

Aunty Di was my father's sister. In everything she did, she was brave, strong, kind and wise beyond her years. She was constantly present, whether it was talking to you, cooking dinner, gardening or walking her dogs. She had an incredible ability to make you feel like you were the greatest person in the whole world, no matter what the situation. She lifted us all up and glued our family together.

I drove from the city back to the farm to be with my family to mourn my beloved aunt. I needed space from Patrick to figure out what to do.

When I arrived home, my family were out, so I went to my sacred space on the farm. I took stock and finally saw for the first time how far I had fallen. As I sat on the soft grass, I looked out at my favourite flower – wattle, my symbol of hope – with its tiny yellow pompoms of golden fluff, shimmering in the sun light, giving bursts of joy and hope just to look upon them, even on bleak days. And even though the sun was up and the sky was blue, the day was as bleak as it could possibly be.

The farm had always been my sanctuary, continually bringing new surprises to delight me as the seasons change. In the winter, dormant blackberry bushes would stop edging their way among the black wattle, allowing their bright yellow pompom flowers to bloom. Soft, red blossoms of bottlebrush would burst from bud swell in the spring, with giant blackberry clusters producing an abundance of berries for picking in the summer. Tall blue gums stood proudly by a dam filled with purple water-lilies, the water reflecting the sky. It had been the backdrop to an idyllic childhood, one that gave me the freedom to explore and discover nature. And it had been the only place where I felt totally at peace within myself, enabling me to go within and be – just me. A place where I could breathe and think and feel, without anyone else knowing anything about me or judging me. I could breathe in the beauty of my surrounds, breathe in total calm and feel so happy that my lungs might burst. But not that day.

I had placed too many expectations on myself during my time away from home. I had thought Patrick's and my love would shine so brightly like the stars on our farm, when at night they illuminated the sky, guiding us. But my light had slowly gone out. My expectations of who I was, and who I should be, felt like a load I had to carry all on my own, pushing me down. I often wondered if my soul would be crushed beneath the weight of it. I was always protecting my façade, always wanting to save face, but the truth was that I was drowning in my own despair and I knew our relationship was not a healthy one. I loved him and never wanted to let him or anyone else I loved down. But I could quite easily let myself down, by not speaking my truth. I was living behind a giant window, like Alice through the looking glass, trapped within myself, wondering if I could change who I was and if I did, would it fix our relationship? Would it fix me? What was wrong with me? Why couldn't I make a love last? What was life like on the other side of the window? Was I brave enough to be my true self? Why couldn't I turn the relationship back into what it was at the beginning in the first flush of happiness before the darkness wrecked our relationship?

I had so many questions unanswered about myself, and so many options in the palm of my hands, but I felt uneasy about all the possible roads ahead. Not knowing where to turn, underneath the gums and surround by the beauty of the Australian bush, I still couldn't find stillness.

Through my time with Patrick, I had withered like an autumn leaf in a cold winter, except that it never turned to spring as our relationship stopped blooming. I had learnt what it was like to live a lie, to become a skeleton of a person. And I had let it happen.

My bubbly, happy self had faded into the shadows. I felt empty, confused about my beliefs and my own potential. I had forgotten what I was capable of – all my gifts and all my dreams gone. I was paralysed by shame, fear and self-doubt. And the more I tried to fix everything, the more my mental health had suffered. I had become riddled with anxiety.

I had lost weight: some weeks I would only eat one day out of seven, as my own self-loathing took a hold. Anorexia was becoming a way of life; a way for me to gain control over something. A twisted way to try to fix the tattered edges of a broken-down, destructive relationship. My body had become a hollow temple. I had bones sticking out in places they shouldn't; my face was gaunt, hair thin and scraggly, instead of bouncing golden curls. My physical being reflected the true inner workings of my mind. But still I put on a mask to hide my real feelings to the world.

I could see the headlights on my parents' car coming up over the hill. After hours of soul-searching on the hillside, all I had was snippets of something I could barely hold onto. My family had so much love for me; a love that was not controlling or denying or torturing. And now they were being delivered to me. Their love was whole, joyous, warm and filled with peace.

God, I missed the peace.

Slowly I walked back to the house by the light of the moon, never once being scared, knowing every divot in the dry earth, every bush that was scratchy, every wombat hole, every tree. I gently made my way around the massive dam and back towards home.

As I walked, I prayed. I had never thought of myself as a religious person. We never went to church, but I had always believed that there was a higher power, a higher force that helped guide us all. I was so ashamed of what I had let happen to me, living in a bitter relationship for far too long. I'd allowed my mental health to decline at such a rapid rate; didn't I have better control over it? I thought I should have had.

Being with my family again as we made arrangements to say our final goodbyes to my aunt, I was filled with grief. I felt that in the way I had been living I had disappointed Aunty Di. I felt like I had disappointed my entire family.

And yet, here I was again, in my family home, on our family farm, where I was continually filled with love, acceptance and support. I just hadn't given it to myself over these last few months or had it been years? I couldn't pinpoint when my own lack of self-worth had started to raise its ugly head. I was ashamed of myself for lying, for hiding my anxiety. I never wanted my family to know just how disastrous I was feeling inside. Though I was sure they sensed something was wrong, and they could also see my physical change. They continued to fill up my cup with positivity, encouragement and an abundance of love, no doubt in the hope of helping me. I am so incredibly thankful for their love; it has been a driving force which has lifted me so many times in my life. This was why I never wanted to hurt them, let them down or know just how filled with shame I was.

I knew I couldn't be the person I wanted to be with Patrick in my life. When I returned to the city after my aunt's funeral, we broke up. I had always admired my aunty and wondered if someday I could be as incredible as she was. I hoped I would have the chance to find out.

* * *

After our horrendous break-up, I wanted to get as far away as possible from Patrick. Far from being free though, I was filled with shame and tormented by all the lies I had told to my family about the relationship. I wanted to escape, to run away. So I went to work in a tropical paradise as a waitress on an island resort in Queensland, but still I was lost and confused as to who I truly was and what I knew I could be. I'd jumped from pillar to post without missing a beat and each rough landing hit me hard. I surrounded myself in endless skies of blue, with turquoise waters stretching out until you could see no further. It was an artist's dream, surrounded by so much inspiration, but it hadn't fixed me. If anything, it had made me worse. I looked for myself in all the wrong places. My ridiculous desire to be loved, a true love, and feel loved had got me nothing but a burnt heart. I suffered flashbacks to my traumatic relationship with Patrick. I tried to numb myself with alcohol but the pain would always resurface. I was no closer to finding my missing puzzle piece and my sense of self was still shattered.

When Patrick started calling me, I should've told him to stop. So many times in my life I have walked down a road knowing that I should turn left, when in fact I turn right, sometimes not understanding why I have taken that particular path at all, but believing it was the path I was destined to navigate, listening to my own intuition. For all my adult life I have held onto a motto 'Everything happens for a reason, we just don't know what it is' – trusting the universe to guide my path. It has been hard at times, almost unbearable. There are times when you think you might just break, but then the sun comes up in the morning and a new day presents itself, with new possibilities and a new understanding of the world: the good, the bad, and the very, very ugly.

I should have listened to my intuition and stayed away from Patrick, but my pain had dulled my connection to myself. Although I was living in a paradise of poinciana trees and fragrant frangipanis, I was lifeless, vulnerable, empty. Emptier than I had ever felt.

Over the phone, Patrick promised this time would be different. I felt bound to him. Like our love was bigger than the two of us. Perhaps it was time to take another shot at the love that I just couldn't seem to shake, no matter how difficult or challenging it had been in the past. Perhaps Patrick had changed? Perhaps I had changed?

Even though our break-up had been tortuous, and our relationship difficult and filled with more emotion than I knew possible, we just couldn't seem to let each other go. For whatever reason, the ties that held us together simply would not break. I wondered why every love story filled with passion often ended up the worst?

It was another hot day in tropical paradise, by which I mean 'sweat dripping down my back instantly' type of hot, when he called yet again for the umpteenth time that week. Sitting in my room, I could feel my make-up beginning to melt off my face – mascara and eyeliner dripping down my cheeks. The heat was oppressive; I felt like I had crashed into a wall of humidity. I took a deep breath and the wet heat filled my lungs.

Gazing out the window, Patrick's voice buzzing in the background, I could see clouds were building over the mountains on the islands in the distance amid the pool of blue. I instantly recognised that rain was looming, as my hair was a telltale sign: a living barometer, it had instantly gone to frizz and my head was now covered in tiny little golden springs. I looked like a golden poodle, and it wasn't even the monsoon season yet!

The air was sticky, I felt sticky; everything was sticky from the heat including my heart. I could feel my head grow foggy. My time on the island wasn't bringing me the peace I craved. I was still falling and I longed for a safe place where I could finally be myself. Questions flew about my head. Would I ever find me? What was I supposed to do with myself? Where was I supposed to be? Where would my life end up?

As Patrick talked on, a surge of energy came over me, blood quickened through my veins. Now was the time. I had to make a choice. I couldn't keep living the way I had been; constantly in limbo, hiding, not knowing what was next, never finding what I was looking for. Suddenly I tuned in to what he was saying. He had been talking about returning to England, to visit his aunt and uncle for a friend's thirtieth birthday. Perhaps if I went overseas, I would find what I was looking for?

I interrupted him, 'Want to book two tickets?'

There was a deadly silence.

'What did you just say?' he replied.

'Want to book two tickets? I'm not going to ask again,' I said.

'Yes, yes, yes,' he screamed down the phone 'Are you serious, oh Jesus and Mary, I can't believe it! My baby, she's coming back to me! I promise you – it is going to be amazing this time 'round. I will treat you like my queen, I will . . .'

I was no longer listening, as I tried to come to terms with what I had just said.

Can I take it back?

Do I want to go?

Do I still love him?

Could we make it work?

Would our time away possibly make things better? Or if we choose to be together, will it be just like before?

I couldn't stay trapped within myself anymore, suppressing everything. But was I escaping one fate to another? I couldn't go back home and live like a hermit on a hillside forever either. I felt trapped on the island, trapped by my life, and this option to go and visit Patrick's home seemed to be my only escape – my only chance at a different life, the one I was still looking for.

But was it the right option? I wasn't certain that it was.

Chapter 2

WHERE CAN I HIDE?

Travelling from the island back home before departing for the UK, part of me couldn't work out how on earth I could have agreed to this. How could I have thought it would be okay? The other part of me, the part filled with hope, thought maybe, just maybe, it would be okay, maybe it really would all work out and our love would be what it had started out as?

I didn't know, I couldn't truly work it out, but something inside me told me that perhaps it was the wrong choice. Once again, I wasn't listening, ignoring the flickers of butterflies that were starting a revolt in my tummy.

I never seemed to listen to my intuition when it came to Patrick.

My anxiety had started to kick in once more and yet . . . I found myself waiting for him again. Soon to be back by his side, and to embark upon a trip to the other side of the world.

Awaiting his arrival at my family home, the day before our big adventure, I was still questioning everything. Two weeks had come and gone since my snap decision to join him on the trip, and I was reconsidering every move I had made and every choice that stood before me. I was unable to move forward, like standing in quicksand and sinking in a life I didn't know how to live.

Patrick was due to arrive any moment, and then, the next day, we would all drive to the airport – together – Patrick, Mum, Dad and me.

That thought petrified me. What if Mum and Dad picked up on how much our relationship had been damaging me? I had lied to them over and over, never revealing the noxious nature of our relationship. My mental health had suffered significantly. I'd tried over and over to fix it in so many ways and became even more lost trying to bring back the love we'd enjoyed when Patrick and I first connected. But the relationship kept crashing and burning and my heart, body and mind burnt along with it. We were too different; different generations, different ideas and beliefs. I didn't know how to make it work then and I wasn't sure I was any closer at that point, but something within in me kept the fire alight for Patrick, even after everything we had been through. No matter what I did, the candle just wouldn't burn out.

I still wanted to protect Patrick. I still had some hope that things would be different this time around. And maybe this trip would be our turning point. Maybe, just maybe it would be the new start we needed. The new start I needed, perhaps. Though I wasn't so sure that it would be.

* * *

I'd been pacing the hallway for the last hour when I saw the headlights of his car turn into our gate and come up the drive. *Attack this situation head on like the woman you are! Oh God, why did I not just cancel and tell Mum and Dad the truth? What did they always say? Tell the truth, the whole truth and nothing but the truth.* All I'd done was lie, cheat and scheme my way through this wicked web that I'd weaved.

Maybe I can hide; it's worked for me so far, sort of, not really. But what other option do I have? Where will no one find me? I raced past my brother's room. Matthew was sitting on his bed. I lunged underneath his bed, pushed all the toys, socks and whatever else was under there and pulled the bed covers down to shield me away.

'Shut the door,' I whispered to Matthew.

'Okay,' he said slowly, sounding concerned. 'What are you doing?'

'Hiding,' I whispered.

'Hiding from what?' he asked, still puzzled.

Patrick!

'Nothing,' I said. 'I just like it under here.'

'Okay, you know you really are weird sometimes,' he replied.

And he was right!

Footsteps sounded on the floor outside Matthew's room – steps of Patrick.

I was terrified of what I was about to embark on with Patrick; terrified of what I'd chosen to do, terrified of how it would all end up.

'Tiff,' Mum bellowed down the hallway, 'Patrick's here.'

No one will find me; no one will find me.

'Don't tell them I'm here,' I whispered to Matthew.

'What? Why? Patrick's here, you need to go say hi. He's here to see you,' Matthew replied, now obviously completely bamboozled.

'I know that, but just don't say anything, all right?' I said, frustrated. 'Please Mattie, don't say a word.'

Matthew leaned over the bed, looking at me with worry in his eyes. 'Okay. I'm hiding with you then.'

'Okay, but quick.' I pulled back the blankets and wiggled into the mess under his bed some more.

'Why are you under here?' he said softly. We could hear Mum and Dad calling me.

'I just need a moment.'

'Are you scared about going overseas?'

'No, I—'

I was cut off as the door to Matthew's room opened.

Both of us stayed perfectly still underneath his bed. I grabbed my baby brother's hand in my own sweat-filled hand.

Mum's footsteps moved into the room then backed away. She was clearly getting exasperated. 'Well, I don't know where she has gone,' I heard her say. 'She'll be back soon enough I imagine. Would you like a cup of tea, Patrick?'

'We can't stay here all night,' Matthew whispered in my ear, squeezing my hand.

'Why not?' I whispered back.

Matthew looked at me, with his head tilted to the side, as if to say – *seriously, you want to stay under my stinky bed all night?*

'Come on, I'll come out with you,' he said as if he knew that the problem was Patrick.

'Okay. Promise?' I asked my brother.

'Promise.' He nodded.

Commando rolling out from under his bed first, then reaching through to grab my hand, I followed him.

As my arms and head emerged out from under his bed, I heard Mum say, 'What the devil are you doing under there?'

'Oh, I was just looking for something I thought I dropped down behind Mattie's bed that I need to pack from tomorrow, and I umm, I got stuck and Mattie was helping me look for it.' I lied – again.

'Didn't you hear me calling for you? Patrick's here,' Mum proclaimed.

'Oh no, sorry.' Another lie.

'Come on, I've just made a pot of tea,' she said, indicating that I too should have a cup of tea.

I stood up and felt as though the earth might suck me into itself. My feet wouldn't move; I was frozen solid.

I heard Mum say to Patrick, 'I found her looking for something in her brother's room. God only knows what she was looking for. She's coming now.'

But I wasn't; I couldn't move. Fear flooded my face. I didn't know what to do, and then a warm hand slipped into mine. Relief then washed over me.

'Promise,' Matthew said, grabbing my hand.

Then together we walked out to meet the man I was about to fly halfway around the world with and I had no idea where to start, or end.

* * *

On the day of departure I got up early, as I hadn't slept a wink all night. I sat on the front veranda with a warm cup of tea in my hands, looking out over the southern end of our farm. There didn't seem to be as many rabbits, maybe they were all still asleep after a busy night, or perhaps they too were hiding from their life. I took a swig of my tea; the warm liquid filled my soul as it slid down smoothly into my stomach that was already churning with butterflies and adrenaline. The tea was not calming me down.

There was a gentle creak as the front door opened, and Mum arrived holding a cup of tea too. She sat down beside me. 'Today's a big day,' she said. 'Remember only a few years ago, we sat right here on this bench, just you and I, with a cup of tea each, talking about your future and what you should do with it, which university to go to, which path to take.' Mum paused and took a sip of tea. 'You know, my darling girl, no matter what you choose I will always be proud of you. I was then and I am now.' Putting her hand on my leg and patting it, I choked back tears.

'Back then, I wasn't sure what I wanted,' I said dimly, staring straight ahead into the open space of our farm.

I still don't know.

'It's not too late, you know,' Mum said. 'Just because you have a ticket, doesn't mean you have to go.' She was staring into my eyes.

Mum had a way of knowing what was always going on with me. How I managed to hide everything I had hidden from her remains a mystery.

'Yes, it is,' I said, still trying to keep the tears at bay. 'It's too late,' I blubbered, now unable to stop the tears rolling down my face.

'It's never too late, my darling girl,' she said, putting her arm around me.

Feeling her warmth, her comforting love surrounding me, I thought that maybe I could just – well – not go. My mother's tender smile warmed my spirit and lifted me up; I could chase my dreams again being back home, being in a space where I felt safe, where I felt like I belonged. The only place where I could feel this way. My father's protective, engulfing embrace gave me the strength and courage to know that I would be okay, and that I could face this fight. And my little brother Matthew would love me, no matter what I did. Resting my head on her shoulder, I started to consider what it was that I wanted, and what I'd been trying for weeks to work out, trying for years really, but had come unstuck at every corner.

'You can just tell Patrick that you don't want to go and you're staying here with us,' she said soothingly.

I jumped at the sound of his name; I'd forgotten he was even with us.

'No, I have to go,' I said standing up.

The moment had gone. I felt like God was calling me: I had to do this.

The last couple of weeks at home, I had begun to find some of my old self; my self-confidence had started to reappear. From my family's love, I knew I could find the girl I truly was, even if I had only seen glimmers of her lately. It was something. And I felt within my being that I would find the rest of it overseas.

'Gotta go finish packing, Mum. Love you,' I said, giving her a peck on the cheek. 'Just pre-journey jitters. Thanks for the pep talk. I love our talks; they always make me feel better.'

With my bags packed, ticket in hand and a giant smile on my face, I was ready. We all made our way to the airport.

Arriving at the airport, I held tightly to the handle of my small daypack, my knuckles turning white with my grip. Heat was rising within my body. My nerves and sixth sense were in overdrive.

Daypack in hand, I refused to be parted from it. It held my most precious worldly possessions to me; things too valuable to put in the luggage compartment, in case they got lost in transit: my journal, my favourite pen, a sketch pad, a tin of paints and drawing pencils, a book, my purse, hand cream, lipstick and a photo of my family.

Wondering around the airport, my sick sixth sense, still hadn't gone away. It felt like an army of butterflies battling within my tummy; it was only the intensity that varied. The feeling that something very bad was about to happen kept raising its ugly head, but I simply ignored it.

Saying our goodbyes at the airport, I felt a swell growing inside me, and I held back my tears as I cuddled my family.

'Take care of Mum and Dad for me,' I said to Matthew.

'Will do,' he said. 'Get me something cool while you're away.' He winked at me then embraced me in the biggest hug. He then whispered into my ear, 'Stay safe; we'll all be here for you when you get back.'

More tears welled in my eyes.

It was Dad's turn next. 'Bye, possum,' he said before giving me a huge embrace.

I felt so safe in my dad's arms, I wanted to hang onto him forever, but I couldn't. I had to go on my own. It helped knowing that my family was always going to be there for me.

'Goodbye, my darling girl, travel safe. Watch out for everything around you,' Mum said, squeezing me one last time.

'I know, Mum,' I said as she burst into tears.

'I love you all very, very much' I called out to them before we disappeared through customs.

'I feel like I'm never going to see her again,' I heard Mum say through sobs as I walked off.

You'll see me again. But next time I'll be stronger still.

Backpacks on, Patrick and I made our way through customs. The feeling in the pit of my stomach was now taking over my entire being; I could barely walk. My intuition was telling me to turn around and to not take another step forward. Go back to the safety of my family. Run and never look back.

But I didn't listen. I kept walking forward and saw a packet of my favourite chocolate biscuits.

Tim Tams – that will fix things!

By the time we got to our gate, I had eaten the entire packet and the sick feeling was still there and getting worse. The biscuits had not helped. I had not said a world to Patrick since we left Mum and Dad.

We took our seats. Patrick immediately leaned back, placing both arms on his armrests. I moved closer to the aisle.

On arrival into Singapore, my luggage got lost. I wondered if it was a sign. Still I didn't listen to my intuition, nor did I change direction. If I moved forward with Patrick, perhaps it would be easier to leave once we reached his aunt and uncle and I had some idea of what I could do next. I wasn't so sure it was being with him. But I was and I was going to have to make the most of it. At least for the next 24 hours.

Another plane, another aisle to sit closer to, the last leg of the long-haul flight to London. A land of dreams, the west end, towers and fairytales. Would my life end up like the fairy tale I had always dreamt of in such a place?

As we descended, Patrick lent over me reaching for his bag, his skin brushed mine and I recoiled at his touch, my stomach lurched and I began to break out in a hot sweat. This was wrong. I instantly knew I could not fix a thing; I could not fix him. I could never fix me while I was with him, I could not fix anything about this broken-down relationship. It was more than tattered; it was severed with a blunt knife; its entire existence a lie. I may not have been able to listen my intuition, I had become an expert at ignoring it, but my physical response told me exactly what I needed to know and I couldn't ignore that, it felt impossible. But why did it have to tell me now?

What was I going to do right here, on a plane, halfway around the world, stuck next to Patrick on the seat within millimeters of me?

Dear God, I've stuffed my life up royally now!

Looking straight ahead along the rows and rows of seats, with the tops of people's head bouncing along with the turbulence, I wondered if anyone else felt as trapped as I did. I was stuck, locked in a vice so hard it was strangling me. I wanted to scream, but it only came out as a deep sigh. I closed my eyes and prayed once more for God's forgiveness for my ability to make bad choices, and for the light to guide me onto the path I needed to find. How I was going to find it, I didn't know, but I knew I needed to find it without Patrick.

Chapter 3

IN A FARAWAY LAND

Heathrow Airport was large. Bodies bustled to and fro, languages from every corner of the world were spoken, a plethora of bags were being wheeled around, people of all nationalities were talking, laughing, crying, and trying to read the signs of which way to go, and some travellers were desperately trying to sleep. It was a melting pot of the world.

High ceilings allowed slivers of grey light to stream through, and stale air was being pumped from air conditioners and working overtime. The place was fast, it was loud, and it was huge! I felt like every pair of eyes was staring at me knowing that I did not belong.

I saw signs everywhere, but nothing was sinking in. I grabbed Patrick's hand in desperation, holding on just a bit too tightly; perspiration covering my palms.

I looked around, feeling so small within this world of transit. I was utterly terrified of being in this big city. If I were left to my own devices, I'd find the Qantas lounge and go straight back home. Or maybe I could just go and hide in one of the shops and wait for the airport to die down; however, something told me that would never happen. *Best to stay with Patrick.*

His family greeted us, I was surprised to see him so emotional at the sight of his aunt and uncle – *did he even shed a tear?*

'Oh, you're here,' his aunty, Marjorie, said to me.

I looked at her in surprise.

'You must have had a long flight, it's good to meet you, Tiff,' his uncle, Hamish, responded, taking my bag.

'Let's get the two of you home and settled in, and then we can head off to the pub. Everyone's dying to see you,' Marjorie said, speaking directly to Patrick.

The pub? I've just been on a long-haul flight. I'm not sure I want to go to the pub.

Arriving at their home, I was surprised to notice that it was nothing like what I had imagined. The council flat in the heart of London had a dull grey render and was filled with tiny little windows, just like something off a British drama TV show. Grateful for travelling light, I managed the four flights of stairs up with ease. As the door opened, the smell of cooking oil hit me. Old 1970s tattered wallpaper lined the walls, with images of Jesus and Mary decorating them.

The worn floral 1980s couch that faced the TV had cushions covering where the holes were. A tiny dining room with a round table to seat four was squished in next to the couch. A galley kitchen sat right off the dining room area that also served as a laundry. Two bedrooms were down the very small hallway.

I then realised that I would be sharing a bed with Patrick as it was only a two-bedroom apartment. I wondered if I could sleep in the lounge, though by looking at the couch, I wasn't sure I would fit on it. Another burst of panic immediately set in. But I hid it with a smile. *Won't be for long,* I kept telling myself.

I placed my bag down in the guest bedroom. The walls were a blue colour, but it looked like the paint had started to fade and was now turning a shade of grey. Thin curtains covered the window. Looking out at the common areas below us, I noticed teenage kids hanging around looking bored. I looked up to the sky. Could this be the same sky I saw at home? It didn't feel like it. It felt like another planet, not just the other side of earth.

I heard liquid being poured.

'Let's celebrate you coming home,' I heard Marjorie say. On the table were three glasses, one for each of them, all filled with beer.

'Oh, you're here,' Marjorie said again.

I started to get the sneaking suspicion that his aunty did not like me. I couldn't help but wonder what Patrick had told her about me – no doubt it was all lies.

'Here, let me get you a glass,' Hamish said cheerfully.

I felt completely out of my comfort zone. And what was worse was that I was now trapped in the four tiny walls of his family's prison.

I was lost and confused and had no idea where to turn to next. I took a swig of the beer. It was warm and revolting, and I sipped it slowly. Everyone else finished their glass in one gulp.

'Right, let's go to the pub,' Hamish said. 'You comin', Tiff?' he asked.

At least I was invited.

I yawned.

'I think Tiff's pretty tired, it's been a long trip. Maybe we leave the girls here and just go for one drink?' said Patrick.

But I knew Patrick – he never just had 'one drink'. I was happy not to have to go along, but then the other option wasn't ideal either, as it meant I had to stay here with his aunty. I wasn't sure that was such a good thing.

'Good idea,' said Marjorie. 'I'll make you a piece and then you can get settled in a bit more.'

Patrick kissed the top of my head and walked out the door.

Not knowing what to do, I asked if I could have a shower. *Maybe I can work out a plan of what was next to do? If I can just have my own space for a bit. But what the hell is a piece?*

'Sure thing,' Marjorie said. 'Here's a towel.' It was threadbare, old and worn – the same as the rest of the apartment. 'Don't be in there too long; the hot water costs a bomb.'

Pulling the plastic shower curtain across, I stepped into the bathtub shower. The showerhead was a tiny plastic one, just like the one Mum used on me when I was a child in the bath to wash my hair. I had to wiggle side to side to get my body wet. The hot water was a welcome pleasure that didn't feel too dissimilar to home. Standing there with the water running down my face, I took a deep breath and sensed some relief at finally being there.

I just needed to work out my next move? Their neighbourhood seemed like a place of death and destruction of one's soul.

'We're not royalty here, princess! Hot water costs money you know, unless you want it cold. So GET OUT!' I heard Marjorie yell at me through the bathroom door.

Turning off the water, I figured I better start looking at where my first port of call would be, and to do it soon.

Dressed and semi-ready for what may be waiting for me, I entered the living area. A bottle of Baileys Irish Cream sat on the chipped wooden coffee table in front of the couch, and next to it were two glasses and a toasted ham and cheese sandwich.

'Is that for me?' I asked absentmindedly, wondering if that was what a 'piece' was.

'Yeah, I told ye that I'd make ye a piece, well here it is,' she said, still fussing in the kitchen.

'Thank you,' I replied and picked it up. I was starving. I couldn't remember when I had last eaten. I ate it standing up; I wasn't sure where to sit.

'Thought we should have a little drink while the boys are out. Why should they get all the fun, eh?' she said, as she opened the bottle of Baileys and poured us each a full glass.

'Take a seat.' She plonked her body weight down on the couch with a hefty thud, and then she pushed my glass towards me. Looking at the full glass of Baileys, I figured it must be at least three nips in that one glass alone. Marjorie started drinking hers like it was water. I stared at her in bewilderment.

So many things about Patrick all started to make sense, now that I was with his family. It was no wonder he thought Australia was the land of opportunities. How could anyone ever get an opportunity in a place like this? I heard running, screaming and swearing outside the front door of the apartment.

'Them's just the kids from the neighbourhood,' Marjorie said as she took another gulp of her drink.

I'd barely touched mine as she started to pour another for herself.

Oh God, what have I walked into this time? Please let me be safe.

Safety was the last thing I felt.

A few more glasses were thrown back and the bottle was empty. My drink was still sitting on the coffee table hardly touched. And amazingly, Marjorie wasn't even intoxicated, not even close. I excused myself to retire for the night, as I was physically and emotionally exhausted.

'But you didn't finish your drink,' Marjorie called out to me.

'Oh, sorry, you have it,' I said. 'Not really up to it tonight, too much jet lag I think,' I lied. I'd started to become good at lying for my own sanity and safety.

'Okay, if you insist,' she said and threw back my glass as well.

Closing the door to the bedroom, I looked out the window and up at the sky. I wondered if Dad was looking at the sky like me. We had always looked at the stars together; he taught me so much about astronomy and how to use the stars for navigation.

But there were no stars in my sky. It was 9.30 pm and still daylight – another strange and unusual thing I was going to have to get used to if I was staying here. Thinking of Dad, I finally fell asleep.

Chapter 4

ANOTHER NEW BEGINNING

People had travelled far and wide for the big event, and it all started at the pub – just for something different.

There was a line out the door to the newest pub in town, with all the girls in short, slinky gear, even though it was fifteen degrees outside. Excitement filled the air as the doorman let the thirtieth party through. The atmosphere was great; the pub was pumping. There was a banquet of food, a never-ending supply of drinks, and a live band playing for us all to dance to.

Patrick and the other guys headed out the back to play pool while I made my way down to the front of the stage with a handful of other girls from the pub, all of us giggling at the cute lead singer.

'This one's for those of you who know how to have a good time,' the lead singer said staring straight at me. He looked sexy, with his rock and roll image, holding the microphone stand with both hands between his legs that were wrapped in tight, black jeans.

'He's lookin' at you,' said an English girl.

'Don't be silly,' I said, staring around and starting to feel panicked. *Where's Patrick? Don't let him see.*

'My names Cheryl. You don't sound too English, where're you from?'

'Australia,' I replied.

'Well, Miss Australia,' Cheryl said. 'Check out the singer; he's still lookin' at you.'

I looked around, checking to see that Patrick wasn't there, even though I knew he wasn't, the boys were all out in the back room playing pool. I just couldn't help but feel worried at the thought of him seeing another man looking at me – the consequence of that had been too severe in the past, I hadn't yet forgotten.

The music kept playing, but the lead singer was now talking to the audience.

'I don't think I heard you. Who here knows how to have a good time?' he yelled out.

The crowd screamed, and I joined in. After a few drinks, I was lost in the craziness of a bunch of screaming girls. I didn't even know what I was screaming about.

'Who wants to show me how you have a good time?' the lead singer said.

Everyone started throwing their arms up in the air violently, like trying to grab money falling from the sky.

He threw a bunch of hats out to girls in the crowd, and then he threw one down to me. It landed perfectly on my head.

'Alright, you gals, come on up here,' he said.

'What?' I looked at Cheryl, and she gave me a push towards the stage.

'No, no, I don't want to. You go,' I said and tried to give Cheryl the hat.

'Don't be stupid. He keeps looking at you, now go.' Cheryl shoved me towards the stage.

I looked up and the lead singer was reaching down for my hand to help me up.

'And who do we have here,' he asked in a swooning voice.

'Tiffany,' I said.

'And is that an Aussie accent I detect?'

'Yes,' I said. *Oh God, what is he going to make me do up here?*

He looked straight into my eyes, and I knew I was in trouble – pupils dilating, face flushed, I could sense his desire for me – I'd seen it all too many times on the island.

I snapped back to myself, remembering where I had come from, who I was – a confident, capable, intelligent, adventurous woman, unstoppable and brave. I hadn't realised how my time with Patrick those last few days had started to shift my ways again, and how he had begun to pull his power over me once again. I could not fathom how it happened; I was desperately trying to stop the pattern in its tracks.

I was thankful for that moment to bring me back to myself, even though I was on stage. In fact, I was glad I was on stage, as I wanted the world to see that I was not the mild, timid and scared girl Patrick was trying to make me . . . again.

I'll show him!

'I sure as hell know how to have a good time,' I said into the microphone. I put the hat on and the band then started playing 'You Can Leave Your Hat On' by Joe Cocker. *Fantastic*, I thought, *I love this song.* My hips moved slowly and seductively, as I started to move in time to the beat.

The lead singer started singing, so I started to take off my coat – the crowd was going wild. Flicking my hair, I rolled my shoulders and winked at Cheryl. Her jaw dropped open.

I slowly walked around the lead singer, with my arms caressing his face and then running down his chest. I then did the same with all the other members of the band. Everyone was screaming and singing and dancing and copying my moves.

The lead singer sang the final line of the song, and I placed my hat back on him, kissed him on the cheek, flicking up my leg like Marilyn Monroe in a black and white movie from the 50s, and then jumped back into the sea of people.

Quickly, I found Cheryl.

'You were amazing,' she said. 'Where did you learn to move like that? Do all Aussie girls move like that? Can you teach me?' She was laughing.

'I've been on stage for years singing. Musical theatre, acting, dancing and singing. But singing is my thing. Come on, lets get a drink.' I said, 'I need one after that.'

I'd made a good friend in Cheryl; we exchanged numbers and addresses. She even said I could stay with her. I felt so relieved – it was a connection for my travels, one I desperately needed.

It was 5 am by the time I made my way back to Patrick's family's apartment. Patrick had wanted to stay out partying with his mates but I wanted to head to bed. I moved as silently as I could, careful not to wake anyone, and when I opened the door to the bedroom, I was thankful that Patrick wasn't back yet either.

That night, dreams came to me of island nights, warm summer breezes, tropical waters and citronella lanterns calling me away, calling me back. I woke with a start. It was bright daylight. Yet, there was not another sound in the house. I was hot; the cat had curled up on top of me, sleeping and purring at the same time – at least someone in the house liked me. I looked at my watch: 11 am.

Then it struck me. I remembered the night before, and that familiar sick and sinking feeling started to rise from the depths of my stomach. Would Patrick find out how I behaved? Instant feelings of fear crept in, and just as fast as they floated into my mind, I pushed them aside. *I don't care.* I felt my sense of self coming back into full force – my performance had relit my inner candle.

I looked around; he was still not back. *I don't think he can say a word about my innocent acts last night, looks as if he hasn't been so innocent himself.*

The shower water washed over me and hit the plastic curtain once more. I couldn't wait get out of the apartment and out of Patrick's world. Stinky hostels filled with strangers would be better than staying for one more night. I turned up the hot water to its hottest and stayed there for half an hour! Marjorie and Hamish were at work so with no one home, no one was going to come banging on my door this time.

* * *

Despite my determination to get away, Patrick started to get under my skin again. He declared his love for me again, with promises of marriage. Alone in a strange place, my anxiety reasserted itself and I lost my nerve. I started to wonder if perhaps the first man that I had fallen in love with had come back to me? Perhaps I had changed him? Maybe the break from each other was what we needed? Maybe we could fix this? Could I fix this? Or had he simply changed himself? Hope was slightly on the horizon for us, again.

Patrick and I hadn't spent much time together since we arrived. He was always catching up with his friends or family. I didn't always want to go and spend another day or night in a pub. I was quite happy on my own, wandering around and welcoming beauty and history of this new land. It gave me time to think, and feel, and work out what the hell was going on. I needed a plan for what was next and this gave me the time to work it out.

I had finally made a decision that I'd travel a bit around Scotland, on my own, work out if I really did still have feelings for Patrick, maybe find a job, travel some more.

Now that I had a plan, there was no time to waste. Packing what little belongings I had early one morning, I waited until I heard the breakfast rustles in the kitchen, to then emerge and tell them of my plans and say farewell.

'Good morning, everyone,' I said as I walked into the kitchen with my backpack on.

No one looked up.

'I wanted to thank you for having me, and for everything that you have done for me during my time here. I'll be heading off today to see a bit more of the UK,' I announced.

Still, no one looked up.

'Well . . . I'm coming too! Can't leave my beloved all on her own, and besides, I'd miss you too much,' Patrick said, kissing me on the forehead.

'What? Why?' I asked. 'Don't you need to spend time with your family and friends?'

'You'll need a tour guide, and I'm just the person. Plus, I can show you all the other places that are not on the tourist map, give you more of a local perspective,' he said. 'I'll go pack a few things.'

Was this real? Was I being fooled again? Or was he up to something? How could I refuse when I had no idea what I was doing? But wasn't that part of the fun of it all? How could I say anything?

A few hours later, Patrick sat in the passenger seat of the rental car that he had insisted I rent, and together we drove off, away from his family home, with Patrick waving his hand wildly out the window.

'This is going to be great,' he said. 'A new beginning.'

A new beginning? I'd heard that before. What was this turnaround? Had his friends talked him into realising that I was the best thing that ever happened to him? I didn't think so. But, I was happy that at least he was tolerable towards me, possibly even loving – he was gifting me with snippets of the Patrick I once knew. Plus I was relieved that I didn't have to travel around on my own.

'Now if you want to get a job in Scotland, you'll need a bank account so they can put your wages in it,' Patrick told me.

Damn it! I hadn't thought of that.

'Yes, I suppose your right,' I said.

'How about we stop on the way and I can help you set one up?' he offered.

'That would be helpful, though it can't be too different to setting up an account in Australia,' I replied.

'Well, it can be a bit tricky if you're not a resident of the UK. You need an address and all of that,' Patrick said. 'We could make it a joint account, and anyway, we'll need one for when we're married. You will have total access. I won't go near it, just put your money in it.'

Could I trust him? I wasn't sure.

I paused.

'Baby, I know we have had our trouble in the past, but this time is different. This is going to be it, our future together. I love you.'

I still wasn't sure. I looked at him with trepidation. And then he gave me that smile, the same one that made me weak at the knees, and I found myself melting again, just like that very first time I made contact with him by the coffee machine.

'Okay,' I said.

We pulled into a town, bought a few things for our car trip and then arranged our joint bank account.

* * *

For the next three weeks, we made our way north travelling from London to Scotland visiting towns, villages, pubs and B&Bs. The land was filled with soul and yet was so isolated in areas. I found it felt a lot like me. Scotland was full of old mountains reaching up to the gloomy sky, with nothing covering them but memories. The smell of dank earth, damp from years of heavy rain filled my nose, and the wind blew straight through you as if you didn't even exist, mirroring the way I was feeling.

Still, it was summer, and most people were happy to be out and about in ten degrees wearing t-shirts and shorts, which was a slightly different sight from summer on the island, or even back home in forty degrees on the farm.

I watched Patrick roll over in his sleep at the backpackers where we were staying. Daylight shone in on me as I sat by the window in our room.

I looked out at the path that wound its way up and over the hillside. I needed to get onto that path; it felt like it was calling to me, to help me find my way. It felt like another piece of encouragement.

I looked over at Patrick again. The trip was nothing like I thought it would have been. That melting feeling had been a once-off and the feelings of confusion and avoidance of my true self has started to raise their ugly heads. His manipulation of words was starting again, and the patterns of the past were trying to break their way back into my world.

I rummaged through my bag and found my CV that I had brought with me. I then made my way downstairs and asked if they knew of somewhere I could get photocopies made, as well as directions to a post office. I also asked if there were any bookshops that might sell travel books on Scotland.

I loaded my CVs with a prayer and posted them off one by one. I wanted a job as far away from Patrick and his family as possible.

And finally, I was offered a job as a waitress in a hotel in the foothills of the highlands in Scotland – away from his family and friends at the other end of the country. Patrick was going to spend some more time with his family, while I worked. And then he was going to look for a job.

In the meantime, we headed back to his aunt and uncle, so that I could collect all my belongings that I had left behind while travelling, which Patrick had insisted I do. At the time I wasn't sure why he made me do this. But it soon became clear that it was a controlling tactic, a way for him to tell me where to go and what to do – again.

I felt like I was swimming in a swamp of the unknown the more time I spent with Patrick, and I was desperate to start a new.

I packed up the few things I had left behind, when a letter fell to the floor. It was addressed to Patrick with Aussie stamps. Picking it up, the smell of cheap perfume filled my nose, making me cough. Turning the envelope over in my hands, I saw the back was covered in heart stickers.

'I'm heading out with Hamish,' Patrick called out to me from down the hall – no 'goodbye', no 'would you like to come?'

'Okay,' I bellowed back. I didn't want to go with them anyway. I heard footsteps moving towards the front door, and then the door slammed shut. I was alone.

I couldn't help myself; I just had to know what was in that letter.

The envelope had been ripped open down the side, and as I opened it up, photographs fell out onto the floor. There were images of a naked woman draped provocatively over a familiar bedspread – Patrick's – the one we had purchased when we had moved into our last apartment together.

I read the letter.

Dearest Patrick,

By now you should have found the pictures you took of me that weekend before you left. Oh, how I long to be with you, pressed up against me. I haven't left my husband yet, but I will as soon as we get back together, and we can run away where no one will ever know us.

Thank you for the money for me to fly over to you. I've booked my ticket. I'm arriving at Heathrow airport and will be waiting for you to come and pick me up as discussed. I promise I'll be knicker-less. You can have me as soon as I touch down.

Have you got rid of that BITCH yet? God how I hate her! Make sure she is gone by the time I get there, honey, or you will pay dearly.

Enjoy my pictures. I'm touching myself as I'm writing to you.

Trish xxx

'What the fuck? Who writes this stuff?' I said out loud.

This time though, I was not at all amazed or astounded or confused. Patrick had planned this all along, but he had outdone himself this time. *Ha! They will be well suited.* I even almost started to laugh.

Suddenly, the door opened again and I heard footsteps. I quickly shoved the evidence under the bed.

'Forgot my wallet,' Patrick yelled out.

I heard rustling around in the kitchen.

Then it dawned on me.

How did he get the money to pay for her flight? He had no money; all his money went on alcohol, which was a pattern I'd witnessed.

I quickly checked my phone banking – $200 was all that remained in my account.

Rage filled every part of me. I placed the receiver down, as I saw Patrick walk out the door.

It was now or never. This was the moment I had secretly been waiting for – no more lies, no more manipulation. I had made my final decision once and for all.

Thrusting my packed backpack over my shoulder, I followed him out towards the top of the stairs. 'Patrick,' I called to him.

He turned quickly, and I was right there, in front of him, as he was walking down the stairs.

Reaching down to him, I grabbed his shirt, pulling him up towards my face, and said through gritted teeth, 'Don't you ever fuck with me again.' I then let go of him.

Losing his balance, he stumbled down a couple of stairs, holding onto the balustrade to balance himself, he look bewildered, not understanding what had just happened.

I walked down the stairwell, pushing past him, kept on walking and never looked back.

Chapter 5

FINDING MY WAY

The evening was mild but still cold. I left the apartment block feeling stronger than I had ever been. I was free to go wherever I wanted. My backpack kept the back of my body warm, but my front was chilly. I needed a place to stay; the streets were not safe at any time of day or night. I'd started to familiarise myself with the area, and without wasting any time found myself in a reasonable pub with accommodation upstairs.

The building was old, like most of the pubs in England, dark inside with exposed timber beams holding up the ceiling. The smell of stale beer and fried food filled the air, which was a scent I had become all too familiar with. I headed towards my accommodation, up the narrow, twisting wooden staircase – it creaked with every step I took. Did they moan just because I was walking on them or the heavy load that I carried?

I found my room for the night. A single bed sat in the corner on a metal frame, and an old floor lamp gave off an orange tinge of light revealing more hideous 1970s wallpaper and a tall wooden cupboard. The ceiling almost touched my head. Rising to lift off my pack and gently placing it down on the floor, I then collapsed on the bed falling into the mattress; it closed in on me, there could not have been one spring left in it. But still, it was a room, dry, clean and safe, and it was all mine.

The sound of birds chirping as the day broke and the dull smell of bacon cooking awoke me from my slumber. Toiletry bag in hand, I made my way down the hall to the bathroom. It was going to be my lucky day – I could feel it.

This time it would be different. I would not let Patrick worm his way back into my life. This time, I knew I had the strength of an ox, and I could do this travel thing. I could make my own way.

It had been some time since I'd been able to shower in peace, without someone knocking to come in or yelling at me through the door. The bathroom smelled like fresh soap scented like the rainforest soap my grandmother used – it must have been a sign. The reflective light from the window shone brightly as daylight emerged, showing the sun in all its glory. *Yes, this is going to be a fabulous day!*

I could feel the prickles on my spine dissolve, knowing I would never be a part of Patrick's world again. The freshness of the shower seemed to start to wash away all the pain and suffering of my time with him. I felt light-headed at the thought of never being in that situation again, giddy like a schoolgirl.

For the first time in months, I started singing in the shower, with a big smile on my face. A big breakfast, a few phone calls later, and I was on my way to the bus station. It was time to head to the highlands of Scotland to start my new job.

While waiting for the bus, I'd wondered if the scenery throughout Scotland would be like what I had recently seen on my journey with Patrick. Looking out the window of the bus brought too many memories back, and uncontrollable silent tears started pouring from my eyes. I looked down at my lap as they fell onto my blue-checked pants Mum had made me. I was so far from home and now so alone. Fear struck, and anxiety surrounded my body and leapt into my chest. I suddenly thought of all the possible things that could happen if everything didn't go to plan.

What if my future was worse? Could I do this on my own? I knew I couldn't do it with anyone else I knew in the UK, as the only other person I knew was Patrick. And that was never going to happen. Fear may have crept into my mind, but my resilience and longing to be me, a healthy me, in body, mind and spirit was so intense like the surge of a storm, I kept moving forward.

Closing my eyes, blinking away the tears, I chose to hide any trace of memory about my life with Patrick in the dark corners of my mind. And instead, I chose to look in the other direction, to look forward, out to the future.

At a transport terminal where the bus stopped, I found a little shelf filled with old tattered books and a sign that read 'Read and Swap. Free books for the traveller'. Another sign that it was my lucky day! Most of the books had tattered edges, some with dog ears, others with stains along the spine. I didn't know any of the titles or the authors, so I chose a fellow traveller's choice and dived in for the most dog-eared, loved book I could find.

Throwing myself into my new book, *The Alchemist* by Paulo Coelho, I lost myself in its world of fantasy and fiction, living the tale as if it was my own. It somehow felt very familiar – a traveller was searching – it most definitely was a sign. Getting lost in a story equalled no memories.

Arriving at my destination, I was ready to start this new waitressing gig at a four-star hotel, as described to me during my phone interview. There was accommodation onsite, so there was no need to find a place to stay. Looking around the village, I could feel the heat rising from the pit of my stomach again – my intuition giving me another nudge that this might not be the place for me. Pushing all thoughts and feelings aside, I took a deep breath, and made my way up the hill in the general direction of the hotel.

The landscape was barren, the highlands sitting in the distance, clouds lapping at their tops, grey boulders poking out of the lush green mountainsides surrounding the village. The town was smaller than I expected, only a few streets with shops lining the pavement.

Cobblestone paths paved the way for pedestrians, between old stone buildings all with hanging baskets of pretty red flowers. It was all so picturesque, like something off the many racks of postcards that sat outside tourist stores. Alongside the postcards was a multitude of sun hats for sale in this fine weather. I started to giggle; it was five degrees Celsius. The wind almost knocked you over. None of the clothes I had brought with me were suitable for living here. *Dear God, what must winter be like?*

Making my way up the narrow, winding cobblestone path, I found the hotel I would soon be employed at, which was perched up high on a hill. The view was spectacular – the water from Loch Eil was shimmering in the sunlight, and little fishing boats were coming in and out from the shore. I could feel myself drifting along like a piece of driftwood floating till it found the next coastline, just like my life.

I turned to view the hotel in all its glory. It was a cream colour, the paint worn from winds and rain, snow and hail, locked to the hillside with no escape from the brutality of a Scottish winter. Art Deco in style, a covered driveway provided a sanctuary for guests to pull up in and make their way to the door without the full force of the weather beating into them.

A porter stood wearing a traditional bellboy uniform. He looked about my age, and I could tell he was bored; there was no one else in sight.

'Alright?' he asked.

'Alright,' I replied. I then made my way through the creaky revolving doors at the front of the building, noticing how dirty the glass was. The foyer smelt old and musty, and the carpet was so tattered in spaces that you could see patches of gold trying to make their way through. As I walked, my shoes made a squelching, sticking sound each time I lifted my foot up, just like the floor of a crowded nightclub. *Am I in the right place?*

I started to feel confused. *They did say a 'four-star hotel' when I took the interview, didn't they?*

I began sneezing from the dust throughout the foyer. Two older women stood behind the front desk, also with the same uniform as the bellboy. One of them appeared to be trying to make herself look busy, while the other was staring off into space.

'Hehem,' I cleared my throat, trying to get their attention.

Nothing happened.

'Um, excuse me.'

Still, nothing happened.

'HELLO.'

'Oh yes, dearie,' said one of the ladies. 'How can I help you?'

'I'm here about a position within the food and beverage department. I start tomorrow,' I said. 'I need to see the manager, Mr Dickens.'

'What's that, dearie?' she said.

I repeated myself.

'Oh sorry,' she said, moving her hand up to her ear. 'Forgot to turn my hearing aid back on. It gets a bit buzzy when the lifts go up and down, you know the way.' She smiled at me.

I smiled back at her and then looked across the hall and saw the old lifts where you had to pull the grates across.

'How can I help you?' she asked again.

Turning back to the woman, I repeated, 'I'm here to see Mr Dickens.' I smiled. I liked her, she couldn't hear a thing, but she seemed sweet.

'Oh righto, just walk through those double doors next to the lift and that's our fine dining room,' she said proudly. 'You'll find Mr Dickens in there.'

'Thank you,' I replied.

Making my way across the foyer, my feet still sticking to the carpet, I noticed an elderly couple sitting by the window looking over tourist maps. The teacups next to them were chipped and stained. I was getting the sneaking suspicion that the hotel had lied about their star rating. I wondered if I should have done some more research, but then again I hadn't had much time to find something else, as I'd grabbed the first job that came my way that met my criteria – hospitality, accommodation, and far away from Patrick.

I stood in the doorway to the dining room of the hotel. Large, round tables covered in stained, white tablecloths filled the room, with dirty chairs randomly scattered among the tables. A long trestle table was next to the wall with marked bain-maries covered in fingerprints, scratches and scraps of old food. *Was this the buffet?* I shuddered.

I took my backpack off, leaving it on a chair. It was heavy enough as it was, without being stuck to the sticky tape-type floor, I didn't know if I would ever be able to lift it off the ground again.

'Hello,' I called out through the restaurant in a loud voice hoping that someone would hear me. 'I'm Tiffany. I'm here for the position.'

'Oh right, right,' said a voice with a robust Scottish accent. Mr Dickens then came out of the kitchen, flustered and obviously pushed for time.

Where's all the other staff?

'We are so short staffed at the moment and have so many buses coming in; the staff have all been working incredibly long hours, your enquiry for work could not have come at a better time, thanks for coming. I'll quickly show you around. You know you've come at the wrong time, we have a busload due in half an hour, or so. I'll give you a quick tour and show you to your room. Then after service, I'll come back and get you started,' he said, rushing his words as if he didn't have a moment to spare.

'Grab your bag, mind, never know what's going to get knocked off in this joint.'

Great – sticky floors, bored staff, and thieves. What have I walked into?

Grabbing my bag, I saw him walk briskly back through the double doors, almost running. Following along quickly, I pushed open the same double doors, stained and grubby up close. As I entered the kitchen I almost gagged with the stench; it was overwhelming. I placed my hand up to my face so I could breathe.

Rotten food overflowed the garbage bins with days old waste. The benches were covered in scraps of food. Food that had gone hard, but not yet quite mouldy covered surface tops. The floor had a marked line around where people walked, the edges of the path black with grime.

Manoeuvring between boxes of God knows what, we came to a back door. The fly-screen door was torn and covered in rust. The handle was dirty and the hinge was falling off. The door slammed shut with a loud bang, I jumped.

Moving quickly along the path I could hear Mr Dickens speaking again. 'This is the way to the staff areas and your room. Get yourself settled in and I'll come back for you after service. I must hurry off before the next busload arrives.' Turning the key into the flimsy lock, he opened the door, pulled out the key and then handed it to me, flashing me a fake smile. Then off he went, running back towards the kitchen.

I stood in the doorway. It was a small pink and grey room at the end of a row of rooms. The whole building seemed flimsy; I wondered how it was still standing. There was a tiny, old wooden cupboard, small bedside table and a single bed. I took a step inside the room; the smell of mould filled my nostrils, just like the foyer. I covered my face again with my hand. Looking closely at the walls, I discovered the patches of grey were in fact mould.

The window let in the bright sunlight, but then I noticed a trail of rat droppings along the windowsill. I stood there, motionless and almost unable to breathe due to the smell and the sheer terror of possibly living with rats. It was deathly still, not a breath of air floated past me. *I'll freeze in the winter.*

A rustling sound came from the cupboard. I jumped – was it a rat? With my backpack still on, my mind was made up. Turning abruptly,

I quickly left the room and put the key in the door. I then made my way back down the hill and into town.

There was no way I could work in that place – I'd probably die of food poisoning, rat poisoning, lice infestations of every kind before I ever returned home. *They should be reported to the food authority, or the police in Scotland, or at least questioned over staff living arrangements!*

None of that was my problem. I wasn't a staff member and never would be. However, my biggest problem was . . . *where do I go now?*

Chapter 6

A COMFY PILLOW
AND A SAFE PLACE

Finding the nearest telephone booth, I dialled a call collect number.

I rang Mum. I needed home, now – in fact, I needed to go home.

Please be home! Please be home!

The international connection sound beeped at us; I heard the operator ask, 'Will you accept a call from Tiffany?'

'Yes,' Mum said.

There she was, at the end of the line.

'Hello,' said a familiar voice filled with love and joy at the thought of speaking to me.

I burst into tears.

'Tiffy, is that you?'

'Hi Mum,' I managed to say through sniffles.

'What is it, darling? Where are you?'

I told her the whole story. How I had managed to get to my next destination without a hiccup. The new job and how I was worried that if I worked there, I would end up sick. And that it hadn't worked out with Patrick.

'Actually Mum, there is something I need to tell you.' I paused. 'All of my money is gone.'

Silence.

I couldn't tell if she was upset with me, or if she was just trying to hold in her anger at the situation. The silence felt like an eternity.

'Mum, I want to come home,' I said through sobs.

People on the street could hear me crying and blubbering into the phone. They were briskly walking in the other direction away from me. I didn't care. I hated this place, hated my situation.

'Well, darling,' Mum said, 'you can't be on the other side of the world and not see more of it. You can't come home and just have gone around England and Scotland and had a terrible time.'

I cried some more.

'Is there a travel agent in the town you're in?' Mum asked.

I looked down the street, through blurry eyes filled with tears, and saw an A-frame sign saying, 'BOOK YOUR CRUISE TODAY with HIGHLAND TRAVEL'.

'Yes,' I managed to blubber out.

'Okay, here is what we are going to do.' Mum had on her no-nonsense 'I can fix anything, and nothing is going to stand in the way of my daughter having a good time' voice.

'Go and find yourself a nice, clean hotel, not that dreadful one you were about to work in. Go and book yourself in.'

'But I don't have any money,' I protested, butting in.

'Shhh. Go to your room and make yourself a nice cup of tea, and run a hot shower. See if the hotel has a laundry and get your clothes cleaned. Who knows how long it's been since they had a decent wash.'

'I washed them the other day . . . I—' I got cut off.

'Wear your bathrobe while you're in the hotel room. Order some room service and have a decent meal. Then in the morning, have a big breakfast, collect all your clothes and go to the travel agent and book yourself on a tour around Europe for young people your age. Explore the world, and meet new people. Live! Tell reception to call me and I will pay the bill. Same goes for the tour.'

'But Mum, I—'

'I'll hear nothing more about it,' she said firmly. 'I have a friend in town and her parents live in England. She has said that you are most welcome to stay with them if you get into trouble, well, I figure this is trouble. You can stay with them until your trip leaves. Though I'm not sure where they are. I'll find out. Now go and find that hotel and call me from your room once you are in, so I know you are finally safe!'

I had nothing – no money, no job and no one. I had no option other than that or to go home, and I wasn't sure I could even work out how to get home. *Best take Mum's advice.* She was right, I needed a cup of tea and sleep, then I would be able to clear my head and make sense of everything.

Little cries of thanks now filled my voice instead of desperation.

'Thanks, Mum,' I said with so much love and appreciation.

'It's my pleasure, darling. Call me soon, don't take too long, just find somewhere. I don't care how much it is, just find a decent, clean place to stay. Someplace where you will be safe.'

'Okay, I'll call you soon. I love you.'

'I love you too, darling.'

And with that, I hung up.

Looking around the village, I saw more grey buildings withered away by hundreds of years of snow, ice and wind. The bleakness of this land was shining in the stone reflection, the same as my heart. I slowly wandered around, red-faced and miserable.

I found a pub, which looked old and shabby, but it had a sign for accommodation. *No, Mum would not stay there.* I continued to wander along the cobblestone paths, feeling utterly sorry for myself, kicking the pavement as I walked along like a despondent two year old. When I came to the end of the street, I had found nothing.

Turning the corner, about to give up, I saw an establishment that I thought Mum would approve of. A gentleman stood at the door with a similar porter uniform on as the previous disgusting hotel I'd nearly become a part of.

'Is this place anything like the one up on the hill?' I asked.

'Absolutely not!' he said with great revulsion.

'Great, then this is the place for me.'

He smiled at me with a look of understanding, and opened the door.

Fresh, white lilies shared their perfume in a tall vase sitting in the middle of the foyer underneath a sparkling chandelier. People were milling around reception with their bags carried by porters pushing brass trollies. The floor was crimson red and not sticky – *yes, this place will do nicely.*

I walked over to reception with my backpack on, looking somewhat dishevelled.

The lady behind the counter looked at me with obvious sympathy; she could tell I was upset. 'Good afternoon, how can I help you?' she asked without judgement, but with kindness.

'Yes please, I'm after a room,' I replied.

As she organised my room and my laundry, I looked around and real-ised how much I had missed living among people who spoke pleasantly to each other and with respect. I couldn't even tell how long it had been since I had been spoken to kindly. How had I fallen so far again? This time, my emotions had been crushed, but not my spirit.

I stepped into the room on the second floor, which had a view over the cobblestone street. A freshly made double bed sat in the middle of the room, with crisp, white linen. Dim lights glimmered and there was a faint smell of beeswax in the air. Old-world relics decorated the room. I pulled the curtains closed, as I didn't want to see anyone. I wanted to be like a hermit crab for a while and hide under my shell.

I opened the door to where the bathroom was. The white tiles in the bathroom sparkled, and there were mini soaps, shampoo and conditioner, and a tiny bathtub with a shower over the top. Fluffy, white towels were neatly folded and a bathrobe hung on a hook. Breathing in the cleanliness, I smelt freshly laundered linen and lavender.

Finding the plug to the bath, I ran the tap, feeling the warmth run over my hands as I tested the water temperature. Sitting on the thick edge of the bath, which was small but deep, I spied one of the little bottles of bath foam. I poured in the whole lot. I was in a daze as I watched tiny bubbles turn into foam. The world felt like it was moving in a slow-motion film. While I let the tub fill, I made my way to the phone. I asked reception to connect me back home.

Mum answered, waiting for me. I filled her in on where I was, and that I was safe and resting and running a bath.

'Good girl,' she said. 'I've got your number now. I'll call you in the morning, your time. And don't worry, darling, we'll work this out together.'

'Thanks, Mum.'

The next morning, as I opened my eyes, I could see daylight trying to make its way through the thin line between the curtains. The phone rang. Reaching out and banging on the side of the bed, I finally found the phone.

'Good morning, darling,' said my mother cheerfully.

'Hi, Mum.'

'Darling, are you still in bed? What time is it there?'

'Err . . .' Grunting and moving my body slowly to a sitting position, I looked at the clock through blurry eyes. 'It's 10.23,' I said, rubbing my eyes.

'Come on, sleepy-head, time to get up, time to book your adventure.' Her voice was full of encouragement and promise.

She was right, of course, as mothers generally are. Throwing back the covers, I shuffled my feet as I made my way into the bathroom. I wondered how long it would be till I got to be in a bathroom like this again on my travels. Pulling myself together as best I could and downing a cup of hot tea, I ventured out in the bright daylight, ready to take the next step.

Brochures filled the walls of the travel agent for exotic places like Africa and Australia. I smiled as I reached out and touched the images so familiar to me – the Sydney Harbour Bridge; Uluru; long, white, sandy beaches; The Twelve Apostles. *Home.*

Two travel agents sat behind individual desks. One was in her mid forties, and the other looked younger, about my age. Both had dark brown, almost black, hair pulled up into ponytails and red blazers on – it must have been the uniform.

'Hi there,' I said. 'I'd like to book a Contiki tour please.'

The two ladies looked at each other and then back at me like I was from Mars.

'Sorry, love, what is it you're after?' the older lady asked.

'I'd like to book a Contiki tour, please,' I said again.

She looked at me, then back at her colleague, wiggling her nose as she was trying to work out what I was saying.

'American?' the younger girl said to the older lady. 'Not English – thank God, Singapore? I know, maybe Canadian?' She seemed to be proud that she had worked it out.

'Australian,' I said.

They looked at each other again, still unable to work out what the hell I was saying.

I must have repeated myself five times. I almost gave up, frustrated and close to tears – not another issue blocking my trip.

Why was everything so hard? What was the universe trying to tell me? Was it sending me a message with every obstacle I faced? This trip had been anything but smooth sailing. It was now clear that if the simple task of booking a tour was to be blocked by language barriers between people both speaking English, then something just wasn't meant to be.

That's it. I can't do this. I'm going home. But go home to what? I still didn't know what I was doing or who I was.

I took another deep breath. *There must be an easier way.* All of us were trying so hard to understand each other. The women were so kind to me, looking at me with sympathy in their eyes; they could see I was upset. I tried one last time to express what I wanted to book.

'I'd like to book a European tour for young people, please. A Contiki tour would be great. Sorry about my accent, I'm Australian,' I said slowly.

'Oh, right, no problem at all. That's what you want to book, sorry. Okay, so a tour of Europe, but what's a Contiki tour?' said the younger lady.

What? Hasn't everyone heard of Contiki? How can I possibly book a tour from a travel agent that doesn't even know that the company exists?

Keep persisting. You must be able to book it somehow.

'We have lots of other tours that we can book you on,' said the older lady smiling at me.

'No. I only want to book a Contiki tour,' I replied.

I didn't really know why I was so determined to book a Contiki tour – probably because I had heard lots of fun things about Contiki tours for my age group. It felt right, just like Mum had suggested. I wasn't interested in booking anything else. It was my escape ticket to a new life.

'I'm sorry, but we don't know what a Contiki tour is,' replied the younger lady, looking confused.

'Call your management, do whatever you need to, but just book me on one, alright?' I was starting to get agitated. There were no other travel agents in town, and I didn't fancy travelling to another village just to make travel arrangements and try – yet again – to make something of this adventure, this trip, which was turning out to be nothing short of a complete disaster.

'I'm sorry, miss, but we can't. We know nothing about this company or tour you want to go on.'

'Fine then, I'll go and ring your head office and tell them that you have flatly refused to take my booking of thousands of dollars,' I responded. I'd had enough of my trip not working out, enough of this town, enough of Scotland, enough of everything! I just wanted to get out of there and get on with things.

I got up to leave.

I was angry – angry with myself for going to London in the first place with Patrick, angry that a hotel like that disgusting one where I nearly worked even existed, angry at the world! Why didn't I just go home? What was making me stay?

I took deep breaths and tried to calm down and get a handle on my own stupid decisions. I took five deep breaths. It wasn't fair of me to take out my frustration on these ladies; they didn't know what I was trying to achieve.

They clearly saw how upset I was.

'No, no, wait here,' the older one said. 'I'm sure we can sort something out for you. We'll make you a cup of tea, while I go out back and make some enquiries.'

They both walked out the back hastily. I heard the ding of a kettle being turned on.

I sat back down. And then I waited. I waited and waited while the young girl keep handing me cups of tea as my anger began to abate.

Finally, the older lady walked back into the room.

'Yes, we can book you on a Contiki tour,' she said. 'There are a couple to choose from and they all leave within the next two to three weeks.' She was smiling at me, so happy that she had sorted this sticky situation out.

Two to three weeks! No way, can't I just get on a tour tomorrow or the next day, not more time here, please.

'Here's one,' she said. 'There is only one seat left, and it leaves next week from London. You seem to travel all around Europe, starting in Paris—'

I broke her off mid-sentence, my voice desperate and filled with longing, 'I'll take it.'

She looked at me. 'Are you sure? You don't even know where it goes.'

'Does it go through Europe?' I asked.

'Yes, but—'

'It leaves next week?'

'Yes, but—'

'Great, book it.

'Okay . . .' She walked away to make a phone call.

I felt pleased that I was finally getting somewhere.

The younger girl came racing in, 'You'll never guess what I found out the back . . .' she said wildly, waving a brochure in her hands.

It was a Contiki brochure.

I was on my way.

Chapter 7

CONNECTIONS IN FOREIGN LANDS

Heading to a new part of the United Kingdom – I planned to firstly stop at Cheryl's place in Durham, in Northern England, for an overnight stay. Meeting her at the party had been a saving grace. I was happy to have finally made a new friend. I'd been missing having friends of my own in my life. And having a 'local' to show me around gave me the opportunity to see a bit more of the United Kingdom than what I would have seen just out of a bus window.

Cheryl and I had got on so well that night we met. She was the only one I thought I had any connection with at all in this foreign land. From there, I would then travel to Mum's friend's parents in Nottingham and lay low for a few days while I waited till it was time to go to London for the start of the tour. It was a solid plan for my future, well for now anyway, and I figured that it was a pretty good start.

I arrived in Durham late in the evening, legs cramping from the confined space on the bus, backpack on, as I made my way to the Indian Restaurant where Cheryl had told me to meet her.

I have always prided myself on my navigational skills. If I go to a place just once, I can find my way back at any time, day or night. Leave me in the outback and I'll make my way home by following the stars or the sun. But on the other side of the world, everything was upside down, inside out and all about. I found that my head had become a scrambled mess of which way was up. I'd had no idea a different hemisphere could mess with your sense of direction so much.

The smell of curry filled the air – the restaurant must have been close. I made my way down a quiet street and bumped into a street sign while reading my map. I turned the map up and down, left and right. I stood dazed and confused. Looking up to the sky, seeing the stars, they looked so different to back home. And then I saw the sign for the Indian restaurant. My shoulders relaxed as the torment of my direction-less existence found some common ground, even if it was just for a moment. I'd found the restaurant; my navigation wasn't so off-kilter after all.

The restaurant was jam-packed, I had to walk sideways between the squishy tables and apologise profusely for knocking nearly every single customer in the restaurant with my backpack. I found Cheryl with her boyfriend, right at the back of the room.

A warm greeting, smiles and beers all round, a full tummy and then the questions hit . . . 'Where's your boyfriend?' 'Aren't you travelling with him?'

My initial response was to tell them: 'No. Patrick is too busy shagging his married girlfriend in some fancy hotel room, which I have paid for. He persuaded me to open a joint bank account and transfer all my money into it, which I did blindly, stupidly, naively, believing that I needed it for my new job. The new job in Scotland turned out to be worse than working in a sewerage plant and when I went to check my bank account details, all the money was gone. He is probably now having a shaggathon with his married girlfriend, but then he will probably do what he has always done. Once she shows she has a will of her own, or has her own opinion, which he won't like, he'll tear her down so that her soul is less than a dark shadow of herself and send her home packing.'

That's what I wanted to say. in my anger. But I was too afraid, so, I did what I always did – I lied.

'Oh, he got held up with his family. He'll meet me further down the line.'

No more questions.

I knew I looked fine to everyone else, but I was not okay. Excusing myself, I raced to the bathroom and threw up.

No, I was not okay.

* * *

As I left Durham and said goodbye to Cheryl realised I had finally seized the confidence to travel on my own – no longer filled with fear, no matter how lonely I was. I could read any bus timetable you threw at me. I'd become settled within my self about my traveller's appearance. I could backpack along with all the other backpackers around England. I was rocking that bus!

Finally, a sign for Nottingham came into view. A sense of relief washed over me – freedom from my past, and blank pages to fill with stories of new adventures to come.

Alerting the driver of my stop, I got off, grabbed my luggage and stood there, waiting. I wasn't sure what I was waiting for. Maybe Robin Hood to come swinging in from the forests – though now it was only rooftops – to pick me up, me a fair maiden waiting to be rescued, waiting to find the light.

Was it rescuing I needed or healing?

Thankfully, light did come in the form of a kindly woman dressed in beige trousers, pressed linen shirt and white pearls reflecting the sunlight, and brown, shoulder-length hair. She looked smart, sophisticated, and had the kindest smile I'd seen in a long time.

'Are you Tiffany?' she asked – her Aussie accent came over me like a wave washing up on the shore. It lifted me up, surrounding me with a sense of home, a sense of peace and a sense of safety.

'Yes, you must be Sandra. Thank you so much for helping me, I'm ever so grateful!' Blinking back the tears just from hearing her voice, I grabbed my bags and followed her to her car.

'You must be exhausted, all the travelling you have done. Your mum has filled me in a little with what's been going on for you. Here, let me take your bag. Don't you worry about a thing. It will be lovely to have you in our home. I've set everything up for you. The car ride is a little over half an hour; if you need to sleep, please feel free. I'll wake you when we get home,' Sandra said.

I was so overcome at her generosity, how thoughtful she was, and how much of a mother she was. I realised then that perhaps I needed her in my life.

Little did I know that it was her who needed me.

The car was a beautiful Jaguar, navy blue with beige leather interior. Two sun hats perched behind the back seats and tucked underneath sat a red tartan blanket folded neatly. It was pristinely clean and orderly, a sign of things to come. Sliding into the front passenger seat, it was comforting after being in the saggy, stuffy bus. The air-conditioning blew cool air instantly as the engine started, with classical music playing softly in the background. Motoring along, we didn't speak much – that uncomfortable silence between strangers, soon to be friends.

The countryside was beautiful. Buildings, streets, trees and even the grass appeared to be lifted from tales and adventures of times gone by. There didn't seem to be one place in the United Kingdom that didn't have a story to tell you. I watched the world go by as the sun shone down on us, my beacon of hope.

Arriving at their home was like taking a step back in time. It was a two-story Victorian manor, red brick with white trims, rounded windows, and gardens that spanned extensively. There was no sign of any neighbours. As we got out of the car, I was overwhelmed; this was the complete opposite of what I had recently been experiencing.

'Leave your bag, dear. We can come for that a bit later,' Sandra said, resting her hand on my shoulder as I stared at the house in front of me. Mouth open wide, like a codfish, I was overcome by the splendid structure in which I was going to stay.

I said nothing as I followed Sandra towards the glossy black double front doors that moaned as they opened under their enormous weight. I was welcomed with a vast foyer with dark red walls covered in gold-framed paintings. To my right was a drawing room with a shiny black grand piano gracing the corner. A few arms chairs completed the room, each low and perfect for sitting in on a long, cold winter's night. Near the open fireplace was a brass trolley holding a crystal decanter with a golden liquid, possibly a French brandy or aged whisky, and crystal glasses on a silver tray. A fresh bunch of pink peonies sat in a crystal vase on one of the side tables; I could smell their perfume as I walked through the foyer.

'William, I'm home,' Sandra called out, making her way down the hall and around the corner where I could no longer see her.

Hastily I followed her, too scared to look into any of the other rooms. It was all very formal and elaborate.

I heard voices and tried to make my way to where they were coming from.

A large man with grey hair and black glasses bounded around the corner. He was wearing a collared shirt and dark grey trousers. 'Tiffany,' he bellowed in his strong English accent that was filled with so much compassion and warmth.

I instantly liked him.

'It's so wonderful to have you here, come in, come in. I've just put the kettle on. We will have a nice cup of tea.'

Sandra was already in the kitchen, pulling out teacups from one of the top cupboards of the very dark timber kitchen. More red surrounded us as we all sat down at the kitchen bench. They were regular teacups, just like you would find at any other family home. 'Best Dad in the World' was on one of the mugs, 'Only love and smiles allowed in Nana's kitchen' said another, and a floral mug with an Australian Waratah on it was pushed in my direction.

I smiled taking the cup of hot tea in my hands, grateful for its warmth. I could feel their eyes on me, waiting for me to say something. 'I'm not sure what Mum has told you so far about my trip,' I said. 'I'm extremely grateful for your hospitality.'

'Oh, it's not a problem, dear,' Sandra said. 'We're more than happy to help.'

'So . . . where have you been so far?' William asked.

Filling in the location details, leaving out any mention of Patrick, I started discussing my trip so far. I spoke about the beautiful scenery, what sort of food I'd tried including how revolting the fish and chips had been in Scotland, as they were so laden with fat that it was dripping off the newspaper. 'Who would have thought to serve food in a newspaper?' I said openly.

They both raised their eyebrows at me.

I wasn't sure if this was a UK thing or just a Scottish thing. Not wanting to offend anyone, I quickly added, 'It was such a novelty for me, I've never seen that before.'

I then started to yawn.

'You must be tired, my dear. Come along, I'll show you to your room, it's in the west wing,' Sandra said, getting up off her stool.

Sandra and I both reached down to grab my day pack; our hands touched lightly. I felt a surge of energy, a connection; I knew that I was meant to be there for now.

Smiling, I grabbed my bag. 'Lead the way.'

A giant wooden staircase lined with ornately carved railings led to the first floor. With hallways weaving this way and that, I questioned how I would ever remember my way back to the main living areas. An array of artwork hung on picture railings over the cream walls. Some were portraits, some were English landscapes, but all were oil paintings with gold frames. Then finally, we stopped.

Sandra opened the door; it was the most magnificent bedroom I had ever seen. Double bay windows opened onto a balcony with a white wrought-iron table and chairs looking out over the most spectacular expansive garden. Roses, violets, delphiniums, poppies and daises high-lighted the green grounds among ancient elm and maple trees. There was a mass of colour in every direction.

Sunlight streamed through the doors onto a king-sized bed covered in a floral yellow and pink duvet to match the lemon colour of the walls. The bathroom strayed off from the left of the room, while an empty wardrobe waited to the right of the room. A small white table and two chairs sat in the corner between the balcony doors, and another window also looked out towards the garden.

'I hope you're comfortable in here,' Sandra said.

'Sandra, it's the most beautiful room, thank you so much.' I was almost speechless, feeling overwhelmed at how pretty, comfortable and homely the room was.

'It's my daughter's favourite one in the house. She always stays in here when they come over. It's been so long now, with her living in Australia. The room hasn't been used for some time,' her voice lowered and filled with sadness.

I placed my bag down on the floor, turning to talk to Sandra, but she was already halfway out of the room.

'I'll let you get settled in then. We'll just be downstairs if you need anything,' she said as she closed the door.

I could hear her soft footsteps making their way back down the hall, as well as long subtle breaths, possibly connected to tears.

Turning back away from the door, I looked at all the beauty around me. The sun was streaming in and covering me; I felt a surge of something within that I hadn't felt in a long time, was it love? And yet this was a family clearly in turmoil – missing their children, grandchildren and the warmth of their embrace.

And now I was with them, instead of their family, filling in their missing pieces.

Chapter 8

ENGLISH GARDENS AND FAST CARS

I heard a quiet knock and a welcoming 'Good morning' at my door. Sandra brought in a wooden tray of tea and toast, plus a small vase with a rose in it. Its sweet scent wafted over to me as she placed the tray down on the little table by the window.

'It's a beautiful morning!' Sandra said in a very chirpy tone. 'Just thought you might like a little bite to eat before the day starts. We've got some ideas for the day. When you're ready, come downstairs and we can have a chat.'

I sat up straight in bed to say thank you, but she was gone before I could say anything.

Throwing back the covers and stretching, I couldn't remember the last time I'd had such a good night's sleep. I knew today was going to be another blessed day. Perhaps I was finally moving in the right direction.

Making my way downstairs, I brought the breakfast tray but chose to leave the rose behind. I found William and Sandra dressed and ready for an outing. A wicker picnic basket sat on the kitchen counter, filled with all sorts of delicious treats, including teacups, a thermos, cookies and salad rolls.

'Did you sleep well?' William asked, smiling at me.

'Yes, thank you, and also for the tea and toast, it was delicious.'

'Oh it's a pleasure, my dear,' Sandra replied. 'We felt that it might be nice for you to have a bit of a break today, so we thought we could all go on a picnic. There is an exquisite mansion not too far from here and it's open today. What do you think?'

'With me?' I asked

'Why yes, of course dear, we'd be delighted.'

'That's so kind of you, but I don't want to inconvenience you at all. I'd be quite happy just to stay here and you can go.' I was conscious of my limited funds, and I also didn't want to be a burden to these incredibly kind and generous people. I was not sure if I should or should not go. I didn't want to come across as if I didn't appreciate all their assistance or that I was using them. I looked at them for a moment not saying a word.

'We are quite sure, and we insist you must come. It would be lovely to do something together, just like we used to . . . with our family.'

I was tickled pink and completely unable to keep the smile off my face. I felt embraced by a couple of complete strangers. 'Well then, I'd love to,' I answered, grinning from ear to ear. I quickly went to get ready, putting my travelling pants and boots back on, but I didn't have a hat. Sandra insisted that I wear one of her straw-brimmed hats.

I felt quite the part as we travelled through the English countryside. Rickety fences made out of sticks lined the road connected to worn, dry stonewalls that marked out territories for properties and sheep, though aged and crumbling in places. Trees were bending their branches in line with the winds that they were placed to stop. Rows of rolling, green hills formed a patchwork of quilted paddocks.

Turning right onto a gravel road, a vibrational sound in the car got louder.

Sandra raised her voice as we entered. 'We're almost there,' she called over her shoulder from the front seat.

William was driving, wearing his grey and blue plaid driving cap, which apparently he did every time he got into a car.

Perfectly spaced poplar trees lined the road on both sides. I imagined that in the autumn the colours would be of brilliant golds and vibrant oranges against a blue sky. As it was summer, the shimmering green leaves bristled peacefully against the summer breeze. The trees themselves were standing tall and proud, and they gave a feeling of elegance and grace.

A long stonewall stood firm at the gateway to the most magnificent lawn unfolding up towards a regal mansion. It was five-storeys high, with walls of sandstone and windows made of square glass panes that looked out over the pastures. Spires graced the top floor next to turrets and chimneys that poked out from the splendour of the ebullient roofline. Elizabethan in architecture, the structure was all in perfect symmetry. Staring up at the estate, it was a majestic sight to behold. Every stone that formed the walls of the building seemed to be filled with a noble sentiment. Every facet of the estate held a regal power that flowed through the architecture and gardens.

Parking the car, I could imagine deer leaping through the forests that once would have encompassed such a place, with wild horses roaming the natural landscape. Now the grounds were kept meticulously, with not a weed in sight. There was a hothouse painted white with small square windows covering every inch, and masses of red and white flowers lined the pathways, scenting the air. My head felt dizzy with excitement at being in such a place.

The day was splendid, filled with laughter, history and a peaceful environment with quiet moments among nature. Relaxing on the red and black tartan picnic rug under a chestnut tree, I closed my eyes for a moment to feel every sense run through me. Sitting with my legs stretched out, elbows propping me up and my head tilted back, my tummy was full from all the tasty picnic treats Sandra had brought with us.

The summer breeze was soft and gentle on my skin, filling my nose with the scent of fresh floral perfumes. I could hear birds calling to each other and flutters among the leaves in the trees that covered the extensive grounds. Taking a long breath in, I remembered home and my special place. It seemed so far away from here. The sound of an Australian accent, the peace and tranquillity, and the generosity that they were showing me was starting to make me homesick.

As I stared up into the trees, I found myself unable to think about anything else other than the direction of my own life. *Maybe I should just go home? Not travel to Europe?* Perhaps it was the kindness from William and Sandra that had brought a piece of me back to myself, one that seemed to reappear when I was supported, loved and cared for. I wanted to keep it with me always – grace within myself.

Being among the estate's beauty, I felt like I did in my safe place back home. And even though it was my favourite place in the whole world, I knew I had to leave it to search for who I really was, to fill in my missing puzzle pieces, and to learn where my place in the world was. However, in the process of finding who I really was, I had lost almost every single piece of me, including the pieces I had already had – like the grace I now felt again.

I took a deep breath, pondering my options.

If I stayed with William and Sandra for a while longer, I could get a job, earn some money before heading off again. My mind raced with questions about my future, and panic set in.

What was I doing with my life?

I was lost. Again. Still.

This thing that I was searching for, I still didn't even know exactly what it was. It felt like I was getting closer to it, as I could feel a sense of certainty about my life.

It was time I faced myself and listened to myself, in that setting, under the chestnut tree. I'd been putting off dealing with any of it for so long, ashamed of what I'd allowed myself to become, ashamed of letting someone treat me the way I had been treated, ashamed of my erratic behaviour during my time in tropical paradise, and ashamed that I felt like I had failed, in so many ways.

In one day, I was forced to face myself, take hold of my life, look at it square in the eyes and start to try to move forward.

I looked up at the sky through the branches of the chestnut tree. Would God ever forgive me for making so many mistakes? I was trying to learn from them but often didn't. What did I need to do to fix this? I just didn't know.

William placed his hand on mine. 'You okay?' he asked.

'Yep, I'm fine,' I replied. I had lied, again. I hated lying, but the truth was too hard to mention.

'You know, I could always tell when our daughter was troubled. Are you sure you're okay?'

William was the perfect father-figure, but was I ready to be parented again? Even if it was what I needed? I smiled at William, forcing the corners of my mouth to head upwards, towards the heavens.

'Might be time to head back then, hey?' William smiled back at me; his smile was warm and gentle, filled with trust and understanding. Something told me that it was going to be hard to keep a secret from him.

In the darkness of the night, sleep wouldn't come, and when it finally did, the nightmares returned. Tossing and turning, I broke out in a lather of sweat, panicking as I sat up in bed, visions of Patrick and times gone by filled my mind.

I reached over for the light, and turning it on, I saw William open the bedroom door.

'Are you alright, Tiff? I heard screaming.'

'Just a bad dream,' I said. 'Sorry to wake you, I'll be fine.'

He looked at me with concern.

'Thanks for checking on me.'

'Alright then, as long as you're okay. Try to get some rest and we'll see you in the morning. Night.'

'Night,' I replied.

William closed the door.

I was shaking under the covers and mortified that I'd woken up the house. I stared at the ceiling, heart still pounding.

I needed to breathe.

I looked at the walls and tried to get back to sleep. But it didn't come.

Hunting around in the low light, I found my journal. I had not written in it the entire trip, which was probably one of the most important things I should have been doing. In fact, I had hardly written in a journal for years, even though it was something that I used to do regularly, which was another mistake.

But this time I listened to my intuition and started writing again. Words poured out onto the paper, clearing my mind. I always found this strategy useful, often finding a solution as I wrote about the problems that I faced.

I'd always kept a journal, from about the age of six. I loved writing and reading. I loved how a story would take me to another place, or how words on paper seemed to find ways forward that I otherwise couldn't make out. At the same time, I found it all incredibly difficult. I'd been an undiagnosed dyslexic. I'd never felt smart at school, until one day I discovered a life-changing quote: 'Imagination is knowledge' by John Lennon.

It always made me feel smart, even on the days when I didn't. Literacy and I had had our challenges. At school, I'd never wanted to read in front of the class, in case I mispronounced something or was just too slow. With these constraints to my abilities, it was only through my passion for stories and sheer persistence that I became dedicated to not letting it beat me. I used my gifts of being a visual person to visualise a world unknown to me, a fantasy land that I would picture in my mind, to help me read the words and turn them into something real. Like a lamppost in the snow, a witch with a long crooked nose, a teenage girl trying to find her way . . . whatever the story, whatever the scenery, my mind would take me there. My imagination saved me many times, even though the words all ran together and the letters became jumbled. Pictures would fill my mind.

Writing was just as tricky, with no idea how to spell anything, I would try and try and try again. I would write until I fell asleep with my head on my desk, collapsed inside the secret pages of my journal. I penned stories of my life and stories from my imagination, with words spelt that only I could read. Pages filled with my hopes and dreams, my pain and losses, strategies and solutions. Pages littered with possibilities. I knew that if I was filled with imagination, then I was filled with knowledge, and that meant that ultimately I too was smart.

And now with my journal in my hand again, I wondered why I hadn't picked it up a long time ago. Possible solutions swirled around the pages with options I could consider to help me move forward. Yawning, I heard the birds start chirping.

I woke up past 10 am, my journal covering my face as I lay flat on my back. Breathing in the day, I removed the problems and solutions that had been scrawled for hours across many pages. I felt lighter than I had in many months.

Opening the curtains and looking out onto the garden, I saw William pottering around.

I stepped out into the sunshine onto the balcony and called out to him, 'Good morning, William.'

Looking up and tipping his straw gardening hat, he responded, 'Good morning, sleepyhead, good, you got some rest.'

'Yes, thank you,' I said, stretching my arms out to embrace yet another glorious day.

'I thought we might go out to lunch at one of my favourite restaurants,' William said.

Oh dear, staying here is going to cost me a fortune.

'Don't worry about a thing,' he called, 'it's on me.' He must have been able to tell I was worried about the money side of things – I've always been a terrible poker player! 'Get dressed; it takes about an hour to get there. I'll come in and get changed and we'll head off.'

But what would I wear? Jeans, travelling pants and shorts were not an option. The one thing I had brought with me just in case I needed something reasonable was my going out at night outfit, and a dress for the party, but I didn't think it was that fancy. I put on the only other clothing I thought suitable that I currently had with me: a sheer, grey tank top that was covered in a paisley pattern, and a short, black mini skirt, adding my flat black sandals and sky-blue cotton cardigan. I looked neat and tidy, not particularly trendy, but it all somehow worked. I put my pearl earrings in, a blue ribbon around my head, and added a touch of lipstick and eyeliner. It was all I had and it would have to do. I was set.

Walking down the stairs, I just had my purse in my hand, as I didn't have a handbag – unfortunately, which was another thing I was missing, other than a variety of clothes.

William saw me and said I looked delightful. He made me grin.

'We'll take my car today. Sandra has gone out to grab you a few bits and pieces while you stay here. She misses our girl so much. Having you around has brought a smile back to her. She thought maybe you and her could even do a bit of shopping maybe later in the week? I told her we were going for lunch. She won't be back until later this afternoon.'

Following William behind the kitchen, we walked past a part of the house I hadn't seen before. There were bits of building material every-where. They were apparently renovating. I couldn't help but wonder how my presence was helping them fill a deep, dark hole that was within their family who were on the other side of the world. But could I fill it? Did I want to?

'Through here, sorry about the mess,' William called to me. He opened the door between two large pieces of scaffolding, banging the door on it as it opened. 'Jolly nuisance,' he said under his breath. Reaching around in the dark he found the light switch, and six fluorescent lights flickered on. We were in the garage, which could easily have held five or six cars. There were currently three cars, plus a black Ducati motorbike. The walls were all white, lined with shelves of tools and boxes all labelled and all in order.

Pressing the button on his keys, I heard the familiar noise and flashing of yellow lights – *beep beep* – I was missing my car.

'We're going to take out my favourite today,' he said as he made his way over to where the flashing lights had come on.

I tried desperately to stop my jaw from falling to the ground when I saw what we were going to be driving in. It was my ultimate favourite 'dream car' – a Porsche 911 Carrera. I had never been in one, but always wanted to. A little squeal came out as I tried to hold in my excitement.

William grabbed his driving cap from off the hook on the wall. I was beaming.

'Ready?' he said.

I nodded at him with my Cheshire cat grin as he walked over to my side of the car and opened the door. *I wish I had a driving cap too. Or a scarf, like a 1950s movie star, oh well, at least I have my ribbon, I'll have to settle for that.*

William got in and started the engine, the turbo sound vibrated off the walls of the garage. My inner petrolhead had been unleashed. *Wait till Dad hears about this!*

William moved the car like it was a silk scarf floating in the breeze, with every turn we moved effortlessly against the tar. I could have driven for hours, the smoothness of the automobile oozing grace and sophistication, I felt like I was in a James Bond movie.

When we reached our destination, I didn't want the ride to end. A gorgeous restaurant sat before us. Once a residence, now a restaurant, a cobblestone path made from hand-carved stone led us to a set of stairs up to the foyer of the restaurant. At the top of the stairs, I turned to look back at the car and for a moment wondered if this was all real. Grass rolled out from the stairway, filled with little white daisy-like flowers spotted randomly through it like a picture in a storybook. The gravel car park was full of cars, lined up like toys underneath ancient elm trees. We were in the country. In the distance, against the rolling, green hills, were crumbling ruins of homes or barns dotted here and there. Trees were twisting and turning from winds of times gone by, lapping the landscape.

'Table for two,' William said, bringing me back to the present.

Walking through the restaurant, I looked around at the renaissance-style paintings with ornate golden frames of beautiful buxom women draped over heather and ferns. The wafting smells piqued my curiosity of what delicious morsels were available to be had. The tables were covered in starched white tablecloths, with silver cutlery and crystal glasses. Tiny little vases with flowers from the garden were on each table, with a tea light candle reflecting in the crystal. The male patrons wore tweed English jackets, and the ladies were in their finery with pearls and diamonds. *Lucky I put on my favourite pearl earrings.*

'Your favourite table is free today, sir,' the waiter proclaimed, pulling out my chair and placing a white linen napkin on my lap.

It's nice to be on the other side of service for once.

Our table looked out over the pastures with the sunshine beaming off the pond by the window.

'The duck is excellent,' William announced from behind the large, cream menu, covered in swirls and ornate markings, similar to the frames on the artwork.

The waiter arrived with two glasses of French champagne.

'What's all this for?' I asked.

'To celebrate,' replied William.

'To celebrate what?' I questioned.

'To celebrate life,' he said. 'And to celebrate your arrival. Sandra and I are thrilled to have you stay with us; it's like having our daughter back with us again. It's simply marvellous.'

I felt my face flush and tears welled up in my eyes. Without any warning, I started crying. Not just crying, sobbing, almost howling, right there in the restaurant.

William was at first not quite sure what to do. So like any English gentleman, he did what he had to do and handed me his handkerchief. This just made me howl even more. As much as I tried to control them, the tears were controlling me. The floodgates had well and truly opened.

Everything that I had been holding in for years begun to bubble uncontrollably out of my body. Keeping it together, never being okay, but always saying I was okay. Never saying a word to anyone about anything that I had experienced – the shame and the sorrow. It was like I had put every little hurt, every tiny part of me that felt pain, loss, and sadness all into a rubbish bin and kept putting the lid on, hiding it all for no one to see or know. And now that bin had no more room inside; the cover had flown off. It flew out the window of that fine-dining restaurant and I couldn't rein any of it back in, not one minuscule emotion.

People started glaring at us. I became desperate to leave and remove myself from the embarrassment I had caused William. I looked at him, trying to say sorry with my eyes, and got up to leave, placing my hand on the table.

However, he instantly placed his hand firmly on mine and said, 'No, sit,' while glaring back at the other patrons in the restaurant. Calling over the waiter, he asked for a stiffer drink and some tissues, please.

The waiter returned with two glasses of whisky and a large pile of napkins.

My sobs slowly turned into shallow breathing. I looked up at William, mascara running down both cheeks and staining the now very damp white tablecloth. 'Sorry.'

William placed the whisky in front of me. Clinking our glasses together, I was glad to take a swig. He even kept his hand on mine, so I followed his lead.

'It's okay, my dear,' he said in the gentlest voice. 'It's going to be okay.' He patted my hand as he spoke.

I took a deep breath swallowing all of my pride and began to tell him everything, like writing in my journal. I told William about Patrick – how we met, how we fell in love, how it had turned nasty. I was still so ashamed of myself, so disappointed with my choices. I had lied to my family for so long about the relationship, about everything, it was eating me up inside, but still I kept on lying.

William knew how I lost myself in the relationship, how I tried to fix it and failed. How I wanted to find myself again on a tropical island and how I ended up in the restaurant with him, still lost, and with nothing.

Our entrée came. I kept talking. Our mains were delivered. I kept talking. Our dessert came. I kept talking. I unravelled my whole life to a man whom I hardly knew, but who I felt safe and secure with. Never once did he judge me, he only listened, patted my hand throughout our meal at random times and gave words of condolence when appropriate. I kept apologising to him throughout, but he kept urging me to continue.

So I did.

The sun had started to set and we were still sitting there, now with our cups of tea, his sound words and advice a comfort to me in my emotional state.

'Stay here with us and get yourself back on your feet. We'll help you find a job. We can have outings on the weekends. Perhaps a trip to Wales, just the two of us, like I used to do with my daughter when she came to visit,' William proclaimed with enthusiasm.

I got the sneaking suspicion that perhaps they saw me as a replacement daughter; their longing for her to come and visit them, or to live near them was becoming abundantly clear. Such kind and wholesome people they were, wanting to have family around them. But did I want to be the replacement daughter? Was that part of my journey? I needed to search for myself on my own without a parent's careful eye watching over me – that much I did know.

I looked out longing at the pastures. *Oh to be free of the guilt and the shame like the birds that flew with freedom beneath their wings.*

I could see a pair of peregrine falcons flying overhead in a nearby pasture, honing in on their prey for dinner. Pausing at that moment, I wondered, *are these birds a sign? Is the universe sending me a sign? Are the birds trying to tell me not to be scared anymore? Spread my wings and fly towards new beginnings. Wherever I may land, it will be a safe landing. Is it a sign? A sign to sing again without fear, like the song of a bird?*

With a deep filling breath, I realised that perhaps it was time I found out.

Chapter 9

GOODBYE, HELLO, GOODBYE

I had just a few days until my adventure departed from London, and I was back on the bus heading north towards Cheryl and her boyfriend Damien's apartment in Durham. Nottingham was a hell of a lot closer to London than Durham was, but after listening deep within myself, I couldn't bring myself to stay with William and Sandra, as much as they wanted me to stay.

I couldn't be the replacement daughter that they longed for. I was sad to leave them, but I needed to be free. I needed to do this next chapter on my own, my own way, and on my own terms no matter how hard it was. I knew that I wouldn't be able to do that under their roof. It broke my heart to walk out their door, but something from deep within my soul told me to keep moving forward, and so I did.

I promised to go back and spend some quality time with them before I headed back home. I had fallen in love with both of them in the short time I'd spent at their home. Their love and compassion was part of my journey, and I would be forever grateful for that.

Arriving in town, more familiar now, I knew where I was headed. Cheryl had left a key under the doormat to the apartment to let me in, as both she and Damien were at work. A note on the kitchen bench waited for me. *Make yourself at home; tea is in the cupboard; beer is in the fridge.* I opened the fridge and cracked open a beer.

I sat down by the fire escape, an Indian sarong of magenta and gold hung up by thumbtacks and knots above my head. Sitting on the edge of the stairs that led down to a dead-end street was somewhat different to Nottingham, but somehow it felt like the place I needed to be.

I hadn't thought much about my tour through Europe so far, but with my departure looming, I began to wonder what I needed. All I had done so far was book it.

Usually, with such a booking, there was an itinerary and a list of essentials, kind of like school camp. Even though those girls in the travel agent had found a brochure, I hadn't looked at it yet.

Cracking open another beer, I found the brochure all crumpled up in the bottom of my pack.

Which trip was I on again? I couldn't remember the name of it. I opened the cover and read some general information – blah blah blah – there was nothing specific to my particular tour. I flicked through the brochure's pages that showed images of young people smiling in iconic places throughout Europe – the Arc de Triomphe, the Leaning Tower of Pisa, on gondolas in Venice – all mostly in summer clothes. It looked hot, hotter than where I was. And I had packed for summer in England, which felt like spring in Sydney.

I see a problem here.

Getting up off the landing, I raced through the apartment, beer in hand, slamming it down on the bedside table in the room I was staying in. Beer went everywhere. I tore open my backpack and tossed everything I owned out onto the floor like a wolf tearing open its prey.

Jeans, travelling pants that zipped off into shorts. Two jumpers, one was a lightweight sky-blue cardigan. One pair of winter boots, winter socks, three long-sleeved tops. Bikini – a last minute addition to my packing, one pair of shorts and one t-shirt. One going out at night outfit, consisting of a black skirt and my grey paisley tank top, one pair of light-weight pants – the ones Mum had made me, they were my favourite item in my whole bag; they matched my cardigan. One pair of sandals, one pair of thongs and a beautiful silk party dress.

But there wasn't anything that would be appropriate to take to Europe in summer, not enough anyway.

'Shit!' I said out loud.

I took another swig of beer and grabbed the brochure, plonking myself down on the bed. There must be a list of some kind, some way for me to know what I needed. Flicking through the pages, I found nothing. Finishing my beer, I grabbed the keys, the brochure and my wallet, and headed out the door to find the nearest travel agent. *Hopefully they can help me!*

The sun was shining brightly. Its reflective light was glimmering through the Liquidambar trees that framed the street. It wasn't far to the local shop, only a couple of blocks, where I found a grocer, a butcher, newsagents, laundromat – *must remember that one* – but no travel agents. I was in the middle of a suburban area; there was just the strip of shops at the end of the street, not the township. *I'll have to go somewhere else in this area.* But there was no public phone booth, no other option than to ask a local. I headed over to the newsagent – the perfect place to get some information.

'Hi there,' I said to the middle-aged lady standing behind the counter in the newsagents. The shop looked just like back home, full of magazines, cards, newspapers and lottery tickets. There seemed to be a gambling option in every country. 'Would you happen to know where there is a local travel agent?'

'Got to go into town for that one,' she replied with her strong northern English accent.

'And how would I be able to do that?' I asked, smiling at her, but also at myself, for feeling confident about asking this question and potentially going on a mini 'adventure' by myself. Maybe, just maybe, this thing called 'travel' had started to have an effect on me?

'There's a bus stop just outside the grocers. Take the 816; it will take you all the way into town. There are plenty of travel agents to choose from.'

I hadn't caught a local bus in the area. I'd only managed to do distance travel so far in this country. I wondered where I bought a ticket and how the whole system worked.

'Can I buy a ticket on the bus?' I asked the woman.

'No love, you need to buy a ticket here.'

'Oh okay, great, can I get a return ticket please.'

Another windfall! I'd mastered yet another form of public transport, and I was again back on a bus – it seemed to be my preferred method of transportation these days. When I got off in town there were loads of people coming in and out of shops and men in suits doing business of some kind.

I immediately started wandering around the main shopping area, looking for a travel agent. However, I started to get sidetracked by the lure of shopping. There were windows filled with pretty dresses and shiny shoes with straps and heels. I could feel the urge to go into these stores to just have a little look.

I even realised that I had lost sight of what my intentions were and walked straight past a travel agent, doing a beeline to the shoe shop. Typical me – I loved shoes. My motto in life, *Life's too short not to buy the shoes!* But this time the shoes would have to wait. I was on a mission.

Four people were sitting at desks inside the travel agent, all with headsets on and looking very busy. Taking a seat, I waited until I was called. I felt like I was sitting outside the school principal's office, not knowing what I had done wrong or why I was there. Only this time I knew why I was there, but I still had no idea of the outcome.

'Next!' I heard a young woman call. She had long, blonde, straight hair pined up in a French bun, and was immaculately dressed with beautifully manicured fingernails that were painted a shiny red. She couldn't have been much older than me.

I took a seat in front of her.

'How can I help you today?' she asked smiling.

I looked around, everyone was smiling – it was the 'smiling' travel agency. I noticed her name badge – it said: Nicole.

'Hi Nicole, I'm hoping you can help me,' I said, and then I informed her of my story, of how I had booked my trip and all the trouble that went with it. 'And so, I'm wondering what I need for this trip, as I have no idea.' I finally finished speaking after a good five minutes.

Nicole looked at me intently for a while, before saying, 'Well, I think I can help you, as we have booked trips with Contiki in the past.' She then frowned. 'But to find out what you need, you should have received a pack from them for this particular tour. Do you know which tour it is?'

'No.'

'Oh. Do you know what date you leave on?' Nicole asked.

'Wednesday 7 July,' I replied.

'That's a week away,' Nicole said, starting to look slightly concerned.

'Yes,' I replied.

'That's less than a week away, it's only four days away and today is Friday,' Nicole said, though I thought she might have been thinking out loud.

'Yes, something like that,' I replied, starting to feel uncomfortable again.

'And you don't have any information on it at all,' she repeated, this time with more panic on her face.

Maybe she can't help me!

'That's why I'm here,' I replied.

'Leave this with me, one moment, please,' she said – no longer smiling – and she swiftly got up from her chair and headed over to one of her colleagues. They had a quick chat, and then she headed back to me.

'Where did you book it?' Nicole asked.

'Here are all the details I have,' I said, handing her my crumpled receipt.

She got up again and went out the back of the store.

I waited. Again. Why was this so hard? All I wanted to know was what I needed – did no one in this industry know what I needed? Was this too much to ask? I could feel frustration building inside me again. Was this going to be another roadblock?

Nicole came back twenty minutes later. I'd almost started to doze off in the chair.

'Okay, I've made a few calls and have organised for the documentation to be sent to you at your current address.'

I interrupted her, saying, 'I don't have an address.'

'Well, where are you staying?'

'With friends.'

'I'll have it delivered to their house then. It should get here in a week or so.'

'In a week?' I screeched. 'I leave in less than a week.'

'Yes, I know, but I can't make the post go any faster.'

I sighed heavily. *Why isn't this working? What is the universe trying to tell me? Are these signs to tell me to stop? What am I missing? Am I listening too hard, trying to make out universal signs, but maybe I am getting it all wrong? Maybe I am meant to just forget everything and go home?*

'Fine,' I said, now starting to get irritated. 'Well, can we at least find out what I need to take with me? In case I need to get stuff before I head off. I don't want to end up in some country where I can't get whatever it is I need.' *What if the tour doesn't go near shops? I don't even know where I am going. When will you learn to take note of things better, Tiffany?*

'Yes, I've thought of that too,' she said. 'I've got a client coming in tomorrow who is also going on a Contiki tour in a few months. I will call and ask them to bring in the travel pack that they have received; it should have an itemised list of requirements for the trip. I'll make a copy, and you can come in and pick it up and go from there. How about that?'

'Can't you just ring Contiki and get a list from them? I can write it all down.'

'It's not that easy. Unfortunately, we need your document first. So I'll see you tomorrow, come in before lunch, we close at noon, tomorrow is Saturday.'

With all my travelling, I'd forgotten about what day it was. Would the shops even be open on the weekend?

'Okay, thanks for helping me.' I left the travel agents and headed straight for the shoe store, thinking that that would cheer me up, but looking at beautiful shoes with not a penny to spend just didn't work. I went back to Cheryl's for another beer.

✳ ✳ ✳

I started Saturday with a clear head, knowing where I was going – back to the travel agent to try to sort out the mess I was in. At the newsagents, I handed in half my films from my camera to get developed from my trip around England and Scotland. I wondered how I would feel seeing images of Patrick again. Pushing all thoughts of him out of my head, I hopped back on the bus again, feeling a slight sense of anxiety for what was about to come.

Arriving at 11.50 am at the travel agent, I'd made it just in time. Again I'd been distracted by the shops; I must have been having shopping withdrawals. Walking into the store, I made a beeline towards Nicole's desk.

'Hi there,' she said in a chirpy voice. 'I've got your list. I've made a copy for you to keep.' Nicole passed me the piece of paper. 'Let me know if you need any further assistance.'

'Thanks,' I said, grabbing the piece of paper and shoving it in my pocket. I was feeling aggravated, and I wasn't sure why.

I found a park bench in the shade and pulled the piece of paper out of my pocket. I looked down at the list:

▫Underwear
▫Socks
▫Rainproof jacket (or small umbrella)
▫Shorts
▫Thick sweater/jumper
▫Swimwear and a towel
▫Pair of jeans
▫T-shirts
▫Casual shirts
▫Dresses
▫1 set of clothes for evenings and nights out
▫Shoes
▫Walking shoes (joggers or walking shoes)
▫Thongs/flip-flops/sandals
▫Dressy shoes (for those nights you want to dance the night away)
▫Toothbrush and toothpaste
▫Bath towel
▫Toiletry bag and contents
▫Aspirins/medications
▫Sunscreen
▫Sun hat
▫Tissues
▫Sleeping bag
▫Pillowcase
▫Alarm clock

Holy shit!

Looking at the list, I remembered what was in my bag. I had a few items covered but everything else . . . I could feel the tears welling up inside me. I'd had some savings still at home, which I was going to need for spending money. But how was I going to get, and even afford, everything else I needed?

I looked at the time. Mum would still be up. I searched for the nearest phone booth.

I made another life-saving phone call to Mum, and once again she rescued me. She organised a money transfer to come through by the following day, which was Sunday – *will it even come through on a Sunday?*

I had to leave on Tuesday to get to London, stay overnight in London and then head out to Paris on Wednesday at 8 am. Time was running out. I would only have Monday to get what I needed. I prayed that Durham had everything I needed to buy.

Speaking to Mum had lifted my spirits back up. She had managed to settle my nerves once again and gave me more reassurance than ever before. I headed back to the apartment with my crumpled list in my hand, praying the whole way back that the money arrived and that I could get the things I needed.

'Sounds to me like you need a drink,' Damien said as I told Cheryl and him my woeful story over the kitchen counter when I got back to the apartment.

'Good idea,' I said. 'I could sure use a drink.'

We headed off to the local pub, which was not too far from the newsagents that I'd become so familiar with. My photo prints would be ready on Monday as well – I was excited and terrified of seeing them. How many pictures did I take with Patrick? I forced myself to shut more unwanted thoughts out of my mind, as Damien opened the pub door for me.

It was now a very familiar scene – old men sitting at the counter with a smoky haze resting over them, booths lined up along the walls, tables and chairs scattered around. The bar was in the middle of the room, and beyond it were pool tables, with green hooded lights, casting shadows over the players.

'What'll it be?' Damien asked as we reached the bar.

'A cider please,' I said.

'Make that two,' Cheryl said.

It was hot inside the pub; the air felt thick. The smell of stale beer and fried food once again filled my nose. It had now started to appeal to me, so I ordered some hot chips as well.

We all took a seat at one of the tables.

'Cheers,' we said, clinking our glasses together.

'Here's to your adventures!' Damien said.

I smiled meekly. *God I pray that the money comes through.*

✳ ✳ ✳

It was now Sunday, and my anxiety grew. I consistently felt nauseous.

Cheryl declared, 'We're going to the seaside. It will be fun. Take your mind off things.'

I was interested to see what the seaside was like in England. Would it be a beach like back home? Or more like the beaches in movies I'd seen as a kid, like *Chitty Chitty Bang Bang* and *Bedknobs and Broomsticks*?

When we eventually got there, the English seaside was like nothing I'd envisaged. A man-made wall had been erected to stop erosion along the barren foreshore. Signs of wind and wild cold weather were abundant. There was no sand, no beach, just a long expanse of cold, grey water lapping at man-made rocks. It all felt very unnatural and strange to me. No wonder they called it the 'seaside' and not the 'beach'.

We could see in the distance along the shoreline a fair overlooking the sea, with white tent market stalls and maybe a few rides. *Could there possibly be some fairy floss?* Pulling on our coats to shield ourselves from the bitterly cold wind, we headed towards the fair. *Some summer this is for them – glad I'm getting out of here.*

Cheryl grabbed my hand and we went running along the foreshore.

I could feel the wind lapping at my ears and hear Cheryl's shrieks of joy. We reached the fair red-faced, possibly from the wind or the cold, or the delight in it all.

Linking arms, Cheryl dragged me from stall to stall. The market tents were a haven from the wind as we entered each one. The plastic flapping made it hard to hear, but we didn't care, we giggled like schoolgirls, trying every product, testing every food item. A photo booth sat at the end of the market. Cheryl and I crammed into the booth on top of each other. Making crazy faces, we laughed as we made memories. We got our faces painted like fairies and took more nonsense photos in the photo booth, and we even went on rides like I used to when I was a teenager. It was all so fun and free and easy, just like being a kid again.

Damien followed along, taking part in some of the merriment, but not the face painting – he wasn't having a bar of it. However, I started to notice that he was looking at me, a lot, in a way that I was familiar with and did not want to be looked at by him. Desperately I tried to make him pay more attention to Cheryl, but the more I tried, the more I failed.

On the journey home, we all sang songs on the radio. We found our way back to the apartment and were ready for bed after our exhilarating day.

The next morning, I woke with a start. Cheryl and Damien had already left for work. It was only 7.00 am. I had a cup of tea, made a few calls, and finally – success! The money was within my reach. Pulling on my sandals, I headed back into town to go shopping!

From all my visits into town, I had worked out exactly where I needed to go for everything. I tried out a sleeping bag in the shop, rolling around on the floor, giggling to myself as I tested the merchandise.

Walking shoes, shorts and t-shirts were purchased on my shopping expedition – I felt like Julia Roberts in *Pretty Woman* after she has success with her shopping. With excessive shopping bags, I couldn't catch the bus – a taxi was in order. I hollered a cab and went back to the apartment.

By the time I got home, Damien was already there.

Placing all my parcels on the floor in the lounge room, I collapsed onto the two-seater grey faux suede sofa. Shopping was exhausting. Damien handed me a beer. 'Thanks,' I said, as he sat down a bit too close to me on the sofa. I moved over. There wasn't much room. I felt uncomfortable – physically and emotionally. Jumping up off the sofa to remove my discomfort, I stepped in front of the fan, making it look like I was just hot.

'What's in the parcels?' Damien asked.

I proceeded with a show and tell of all my purchases, showing much more enthusiasm about my trip than I felt. I was then beginning to feel awkward around Damien, as something about him just wasn't adding up, and getting involved in another couple's troubles was the last thing I needed.

I heard the keys in the door. *Thank God* – Cheryl was home.

'What are you doing home?' she asked briskly.

'Got an early mark,' Damien replied coldly.

I raced over to her and embraced her. 'Welcome home, Cheryl. Let me get you a drink.' Relief rushed through me at the sight of her.

Something was definitely up between them, and I knew it. I was starting to think I should have stayed with William and Sandra.

'Make it a cider. It's bloody hot,' Cheryl called as she made her way over to the fan.

Walking back into the lounge room, I heard the phone ring. Cheryl took the drink from my hand as she answered the phone and went into the kitchen.

'Who is it?' Damien yelled across the lounge room.

Cheryl came back in with a look of betrayal and disappointment on her face.

'Who was that?' Damien asked again.

'No one, telemarketers,' Cheryl replied.

Something told me that Cheryl was lying. I knew only too well how to hide the truth, and now I was able to tell when others were using my secret weapon – a lie.

We all enjoyed a few more beers, and then we ordered in Indian. It was way too hot to cook, and too hot to go out. We all piled around the pedestal fan, taking turns in front of it. The sudden change in temperatures were nothing like I had experienced back home, I wasn't used to such erratic weather.

I needed a huge rest before the next leg of the journey. Excusing myself, I went off to bed.

I started to throw all my shopping bags in the corner when I heard a knock at the door.

Oh no, please don't be Damien.

'Hello, can I come in?' It was Cheryl.

'Sure,' I replied with a heavy sigh of relief.

Cheryl opened the door. I was perched up on the bed, trying to pry open the windows, perspiration dripping down my forehead.

'It won't work. They have been painted shut.'

'Bother,' I replied as the perspiration then dripped down my back.

Cheryl sat down on the floor, looking at all my shopping bags, all piled in a heap.

'It must be nice to be so free,' Cheryl said looking at the bags.

If only she knew the reasons behind my story. I paused, almost forgetting to breathe.

'What's this?' she asked, picking up the stack of photos I'd had picked up from the newsagent on my way to the shops.

I'd purposely decided not to show them any of the photos. I hadn't even looked at them myself. I couldn't.

Cheryl looked through them in detail, one by one – some of Scotland, mostly of the landscape, but some images of Patrick, and one of us where we are both smiling. When I looked at it I could see the strain in both of our eyes – a forced smile with sadness leaking out of the corners of my eyes.

'It's a beautiful photo of the two of you,' she said.

I said nothing. What could I say? It felt like he had ruined a part of my life, a part of me. But I was slowly coming out of the flames – still vulnerable, still hiding, still trying to bring myself back to the real me.

Cheryl got up to leave.

'Thanks again for letting me stay.'

'It's no problem at all,' she said, smiling and closing the door behind her.

I felt like I had been shot with an arrow straight into my soul seeing the photos of Patrick and me. My stomach churned, breaking into spasms of knots. Bending over in pain, I raced to the bathroom and vomited. Pulling myself together, I threw away the photos.

Finishing my packing, I heard voices yelling and cursing at each other; they were getting louder. I looked down at the street. I couldn't see anyone, only the light of the moon on this crystal-clear night shining down on the earth.

I slowly opened my door – was it Cheryl and Damien?

'Who is Evelyn? Why is she calling you?' Cheryl screamed at Damien.

I closed the door again, jumped into bed, turned the lights out and put the pillow over my head, shaking. The sound of a raised voice instantly surged fear into me.

Laying their paralysed, my breathing started to become shallow. I couldn't think straight, nor move. I was frozen on the bed; fear and anxiety consumed my every muscle. My eyes were wider than saucers, filled with terror at what lay ahead, waiting for the door to come slamming open.

The voices died down; I heard crying. But no footsteps were headed my way. I waited, shaking underneath the covers.

I finally drifted off to sleep and awoke in the early hours of the morning. I found my body stiff and sore from the adrenaline rush that had gone through me. I couldn't stay, not another minute. My fight or flight response kicked in; I choose flight.

I left the room neat and tidy, just how I'd found it. With my bag on my back again, I wrote a note to Cheryl and Damien thanking them for all their hospitality, for their friendship and help. I left the note, apartment key, and some money on the kitchen bench to help pay for any outstanding items, and then I quietly snuck out the door before either of them woke up.

Chapter 10

NOT A STAR IN THE SKY

It was raining as I made my way to the bus stop, and the one item I had decided not to purchase was a raincoat! My new straw hat proceeded to get wet from the early morning summer rain. By the time I was on the bus, it was a sloppy floppy, no-shape hat that fell over my face, and I couldn't see through it – what a waste – I threw it in the bin. I wasn't taking anything I didn't need with me, and I didn't need a sloppy hat.

There was a post office right across the road from the bus depot. I had bundled up some of my bits and pieces to send back home, putting them in one of my shopping bags. I didn't need to take with me my art kit or my beautiful silk dress.

Walking out of the post office, I saw a bus departing. Looking at my watch, it showed that it was only 9.05 am, I'd only taken five minutes at the post office, and my bus wasn't due to leave until 9.15 am – I had plenty of time. I looked up at the bus as it was pulling out of the driveway. The destination sign said 'London'.

Hmm, that's funny. I thought there was only one bus in the morning departing for London.

Walking back to the terminal, I asked the man behind the ticket booth when the next bus to London was due to leave. 'Is it in the next ten minutes?' I enquired.

'No, love, you've just missed it. It left right on time, 9.15 am,' replied the man behind the booth.

'What?' I shrieked – panic started to rise up inside me. 'But I . . . I . . .' I started stuttering. 'It's only 9.05 now.'

Hang on – it was 9.05, five minutes ago, when I left the post office. *What's going on?* I held my watch up to my ear. No noise.

'No, miss, it's now 9.30, and we're very proud of our buses travelling right on schedule,' he replied once more, sounding very proud of himself and the company he worked for.

'Are you trying to kill me?' I yelled looking up at the sky, at God. My watch had stopped, right at 9.05. I couldn't believe it.

'Well, when is the next bus?' I asked, staring back at the man, breathless, heart racing and anxiety starting to overcome me. My neck felt hot with the instant rush of blood flow. I thought my head might explode.

'Noon.'

A line had started to build up behind me. I didn't care; I needed to think straight, wondering if I would make it in time to check into the hotel and get sorted before I got on the bus tomorrow for Paris.

'How long to get to London on the noon bus?' I asked, aware of the lady behind me getting increasingly frustrated with my inability to make a quick decision.

'Oh, miss, it's a long trip that one, many stops, there is a stop-over halfway, let me recheck the timetable.'

The woman behind me kept muttering to herself under her breath as the ticket officer tried to help me work out my next plan.

'Says here you'll get in at about 9 pm, but if the traffic is heavy, it could be 10 pm.'

'Is there nothing quicker?' I responded with desperation in my voice.

'Well, you could get the train. I'll just check the timetable.'

The muttering from behind me from my fellow traveller was getting louder; there was now an element of deep sighs as well.

'Sorry, missus, you've missed that one too. Nothing till tomorrow now.'

'Fuck! Okay, right, sorry,' I said, apologising to the ticket officer, who now was also acutely aware of the growing line of passengers waiting to get their tickets.

'Oh, make a decision for fuck's sake,' said the woman behind me. She had purple hair and gothic makeup, and was wearing a lace dress in black and purple. She smelt like incense.

I turned to look at her; I was in no mood to deal with anyone's rudeness. 'You will get your turn all in good time, but I was here first, and I intend to work out my dire situation with this good-willed ticket officer before I let any of you get your turn . . .' I was now talking very loudly, pointing at the entire line. 'My life is in ruins, and I need to sort some shit out, so if you don't mind, get off my back. I'll be done soon, and then you can have your turn, or simply fuck off.'

I had had enough of everything. Frustrated and angry, I was on the verge of a complete meltdown – again. I turned back to the ticket officer; he now looked at me a little bit more on the scared side than the frustrated side.

'Can I get to London on the ticket I already have?' I asked him politely.

'Not usually, but I'll make an allowance for you,' he said as he handed me another ticket.

'Thank you,' I said, turning around and making my way to the waiting area for passengers. I didn't look at the now very long line. And luckily, no one said anything to me as I walked away. When I sat down, I threw my pack on the ground with force, grabbed a chocolate bar out of my daypack and sat there eating it, staring into space. Reaching back into my daypack, I found the book that I had been reading on another bus, on another day with another adventure lurking ahead of me. I grabbed that and started reading it, hoping for some divine inspiration.

Noon came and went; yet still the bus had not arrived.

I went back up to the ticket office. The shift times must have changed; it was a woman this time, she had a tattoo running up her neck, bright red lipstick, dark brown haunting eyes and a crew cut hairstyle died pink on top. She looked like she wouldn't take any nonsense, just like how I felt inside.

'Um, hi there,' I said.

'What do ya want?' she replied, not looking up from her gossip magazine.

'Do you know if the noon bus to London is on its way?'

'Been held up.'

'Oh,' I responded. *So much for running on time.*

'Do you have any idea when it will be arriving?' I asked.

'Nope,' she replied, still looking down at her magazine.

I walked away. What could I do? Sitting back down, I continued to wait. Luckily they had a vending machine in the terminal; I was living on crisps and chocolate.

At 4 pm, the bus titled LONDON came through the gates. 'Oh, thank God,' I muttered under my breath, as a sense of relief flooded over me. *At this rate, I should get into London by midnight. Reception shuts at 10 pm. Shit. Well, if there is no night manager, I'll just have to sleep out on the doorstep, what choice do I have?*

Climbing on board the bus, I took a long, deep breath, rested my head on my daypack by the window and fell asleep.

I awoke to a sudden jerk. Looking out the window, it was night, streetlights were on, and the sky was black. It was an overcast night with not a star in the sky. The bus diver announced that he was hungry and that we were stopping to refuel and grab a bite to eat.

No wonder it was so late in the first place, if he is choosing his own timetable. You're not going to stay in this job much longer, mate.

I walked into the petrol station. Dried-up old sandwiches and a bowl of fruit that looked like it had been there for a month with flies floating all around it sat on the counter. *Not very appetising.* I wandered around the petrol station. It had to be one of the filthiest I had ever been too. There was a queue for the ladies restrooms; I'd get something to eat first, and then go once the line had lessened a bit.

I bought another chocolate bar and a Coke, as I thought that that was my safest bet. In fact, I got two chocolate bars. And then I lined up in the queue for the restroom. Once in, I held my breath; someone had vomited all over the walls. It was worse than a public toilet in a park. I reached into my pack and found some tissues, being careful not to touch anything. On leaving, I went back to the counter and informed the attendant of the state of the bathrooms.

'This ain't fucking Buckingham Palace, be glad you could take a piss.'

I looked at him in shock and walked out of the shop. I then asked the driver if I could grab my backpack, others too wanted to get items from below the bus. I found some soap in my bag and washed the hell out of my hands with the outside tap.

The stop had delayed us by at least an hour; it was now 8 pm. *I have plenty of time.*

Slowly the bus started to become empty, with the bus stopping at what seemed like every second corner. I drifted in and out of sleep until eventually the bright lights from outside prevented me from closing my eyes again. We had finally arrived.

I was in London.

There were cars everywhere; the traffic was bumper to bumper. Black taxis filled the streets, and people were jammed in like a pack of sardines as they walked along the footpaths, spilling out and onto the road. The classic double-decker red buses beeped their horns as they made their way through narrow streets, looking like they may tumble over as they turned a corner. I felt like I was on a movie set, watching the extras bumbling their way around.

I forgot how big London was; it felt almost alien-like, the busyness of the streets, the masses of people, and the traffic. Sydney was nowhere near as busy as London. Anxiety filled my lungs. I closed my eyes, as I couldn't take in anymore sights for one day. I was exhausted, emotionally wrecked, and I had no intention of filling up my mind with more visions tonight.

The bus pulled into Victoria Station and only two of us got off the bus. I must have slept nearly the whole trip; I hadn't realised that everyone else had already got off, not that I cared. All I needed now was to find my way to the hotel. Grabbing my pack, I looked up at the clock; it was 1.40 am. *How on earth had the trip taken so long?* The bus driver locked up, and I looked around and saw no one.

Half asleep and still bleary-eyed, I started to make my way out towards the street. *There must be a taxi rank nearby?* By the time I reached the road, all the lights of the terminal had been turned off. Victoria Bus Station had closed for the night.

I stood at the edge of the street, which had turned out to be an alleyway. I must have taken a wrong turn somewhere in my half-asleep state. I stood there looking around. *Which way to go?* I couldn't turn back, as everything was closed and dark, and the roller shutters had all been pulled down. I had nowhere else to go but left or right, up or down the alleyway. The streetlights were dim; the smell of bus fumes and smog filled my lungs. I found it hard to breathe.

I looked to my right and saw two large figures coming towards me from the top of the alleyway. It looked like two men, but I couldn't make out their faces. However, their walk made me nervous. I did not like where this was headed.

I looked to my left – it was a dead-end street.

Heart racing, I wondered what on earth I should do – maybe find a bench somewhere by Victoria Station? But I hadn't seen one as I'd walked through, and the entrance was now closed. If I went right, my intuition told me that there was a possibility of being raped, robbed, beaten or even murdered. Things had gone from bad to worse – there was not another soul around. I stood there a moment longer, wondering what on earth I was going to do.

I looked to my right again, when I heard a noise behind me – a girl about my age appeared out of nowhere.

'What are you doing here?' she asked sounding fearful.

'Trying to work out how to get to my hotel,' I said honestly, palms sweating but thankful that there were now two of us. *Safety in numbers.*

'Oh, you're Australian,' she said. 'Come with me.' She grabbed my arm and quickly lead me across the road.

I figured I had no choice; she was a better option than the two scary men coming towards me in a dark alleyway in the middle of the night in London. She opened the door to a pewter-coloured Mercedes Benz.

The girl scooted across the seat and motioned for me to come in too. 'Quick,' she said and reached over me, locking the door. She helped me pull my pack off, and then after dumping it between us, she told the driver to 'Go!'

He took off at high speed.

The driver was an older gentleman, with short-styled grey hair. I couldn't see his face from the back passenger seat, but he looked like he was about the size of a Rugby Union player. I couldn't help but wonder what an older gentleman driving a Mercedes Benz was doing at a bus station in the middle of the night, but I was grateful for the comfortable ride.

The girl next to me started to talk. 'It's okay, you can trust me.' I must have looked fearful. 'It's not a good idea to be on the streets alone at this time of night, especially in dark alleyways, but you already knew that right?' she said giggling. 'Where are you going anyway? And what were you doing all alone at Victoria Station. It's not a safe place, you know?' She hardly drew a breath as she spoke. 'I love Australians. My boyfriend is Australian. He's from Sydney. He's a musician, and he plays the guitar. Do you play an instrument?'

The girl eventually stopped talking and stared at me, waiting on the edge of the car seat to hear all my answers.

'I'm going on a tour tomorrow, on a Contiki tour through Europe. I've got to get to the hotel tonight to leave first thing in the morning.' I pulled a piece of crumpled paper out of my pocket; another detail the travel agent had given me.

The girl looked at the piece of paper. 'Oh, I know where that is. Gary, she's going to the Royal National Hotel in Russell Square.'

'On it,' Gary said, with a broad English accent – at least I now knew the name of the driver, but I still didn't know the girl's name.

'How do you know it?' I asked, still perplexed as to how I had found her and why she knew where I was going.

'Oh, I know lots of places,' she said smiling at me.

'By the way, I'm Tiffany,' I said.

'Hi Tiffany, I'm Penelope, but everyone calls me Penny,' replied the girl. Her blue eyes twinkled as she spoke.

'Everyone calls me Tiff,' I said. 'I used to have a dog called Penny.'

I suddenly felt a longing for home, instead of being in this stinky city, in yet another posh car, with strangers that had saved my arse – again.

'How did you end up being at Victoria Station too,' I asked, wondering how I had ended up in this car in the first place.

'My boyfriend had a gig on not far from there, and I often get Gary to drive me around, as it's much safer that way. Hey, we're almost there. When you get back, you should come and stay with us. We have a spare room, and my boyfriend is totally fine with other Aussies coming to stay, it will be heaps of fun, you can get a job in one of the pubs nearby like all the other backpackers do, and we can become lifelong friends.'

She grabbed a piece of paper out of the door of the car and a pen and scribbled down her address, her name and phone number. 'When you get back, they'll drop you at Russell Square. It's expensive to stay there, give me a call straight away. I'll come pick you up with Gary and you can stay with us, for as long as you like.' Penny was so kind. I even considered her offer. She was like a guardian angel coming out of nowhere at the bus depot. *Maybe we would become lifelong friends.*

We pulled up outside the Royal National Hotel. I saw a Contiki flag blowing in the breeze, poking out from the grey building that was the hotel. It looked anything but Royal.

'How much do I owe you, Gary?' I asked

'Whatever you think is reasonable,' he replied.

What? I have no idea what is reasonable. So I handed over five pounds. 'Thanks, Gary.'

He took the money and smiled, saying nothing. Was it not enough or too much? I couldn't read his response. Too tired to care, I had other things on my mind, like how I was going to check into my room when reception closed at 10 pm!

Grabbing my bag, Penny gave me an embracing hug goodbye. She called out as they drove off, 'See you in a month!' and waved her arms frantically out the window. And then, she was gone.

Looking up at the grey, 1970s building, I thought it looked like a back-packers hotel – thanks to the pokey rectangular windows, most of them with the curtains closed, all in vertical and horizontal lines surrounded by grey concrete. International flags hung across the top of the foyer entrance: Canada, America, Germany, Australia and Japan. The flags waved slowly in the limited breeze. The air was oppressive, stifling almost, even though I was outside – this city wasn't designed for hot temperatures.

It was the most depressing-looking hotel I had ever seen. The guttering was even falling off over the foyer entrance, and the dirty windows by the entrance showed no sign of life anywhere. *Will I even be able to get in? Or am I destined to sleep on the filthy, blue, plastic chairs that surround the smoking area?*

I slowly made my way towards the double-glass automatic doors. A sign was posted up on the door that said: *If checking in after hours, please press the buzzer to your left. If there are any prank calls, the police will be called.*

I rang the buzzer.

'Hi, sorry to wake you,' I said into the intercom, which was nestled into the wall and surrounded with duct tape – someone had tried to rip it out of the wall at some point by the look of things, and this was their attempt to fix it.

'I'm Tiffany. I've got a room booked for tonight. Sorry to get in so late,' I spoke into the intercom.

'Yes, we've been expecting you. I'll come down right away. Let yourself in,' responded the voice from the intercom – at least it worked, even though it looked derelict.

The doors buzzed and I walked in. The reception area was basic – white tiles lined the floor, and wooden panels lined the base of the reception area that was lit up with images of London, Big Ben and Buckingham Palace. I could hear music and people singing; it must have been coming from a bar somewhere in the hotel.

A side door opened behind reception, and what must have been the night-duty manager walked in, still in his black suit and tie. I was impressed, though I couldn't see underneath the desk. *He might have his pyjama bottoms on.* A smirk appeared on my face.

'You must be Tiffany,' he said, looking at me with pity.

I must have looked dishevelled. The trip had been longer than I anticipated and the last few days had taken their toll on me. I needed a shower. I needed a good nights sleep. And I needed a decent meal.

'You're in room 457. Here are your keys, breakfast is between 6 and 10 am and served in the restaurant just across from us. Your bus leaves at 8 am. You will need to be all packed and ready to go by seven thirty. Lifts are along the corridor and to your left.'

97

'Great, thanks,' I said taking the keys.

I longed for a comfortable bed, a room all to myself, with a hot shower. My body was weary, and my mind was even more exhausted. Maybe the room would have a kettle and a tea bag, and possibly a lovely teacup too – I was in London after all, the land of tea drinkers. I stood in the elevator with a heavy weight on my back and within my soul.

The doors to the elevator opened on my floor; I was moments away from the best sleep of my life. I possibly wouldn't even make it to the kettle, just merely fall face first onto the bed, not even lifting my backpack off, waking in the morning feeling refreshed before the next step.

The sound of laughter and yahoos greeted me as I stepped into the hallway.

'Oh, God, no,' I said out loud, standing in the hallway. I'd landed on the party floor. I guessed that everyone was staying or returning from a trip and ready for a good time. *Damn it – I should have thought about that.*

I tentatively headed down the hall and passed the rooms – 454: the noise was getting louder, 456: louder, 457: my door, to my room, my room with no one else in there?

However, opening the door to my room, I quickly realised that it wasn't just 'my' room. It was a shared room, with three others – it was a room for four. My bed was still perfectly made at the end of the room, with two girls sitting on it drinking beer.

What?

I hadn't checked the details of my check-in, too tired to care, too emotional when I booked it, and I had gone with the cheapest option. And now standing in the doorway, with a bunch of young girls around my age stopping dead in their tracks, staring at me, I remembered I'd ticked 'shared room'.

Shit.

'Hi,' I said in a weak voice.

'What are you doing here?' said one of the girls with long, straight, brown hair, wearing a crown of sorts made out of socks.

'I'm bunking in with you guys, just for tonight. I head out tomorrow.'

'So do we,' said one of the girls sitting on the bed that was obviously meant for me.

'You mean you just got in, like now?' said the other girl, also sitting on my bed.

They looked so young – did I appear that young? I didn't feel young. I felt tired and older somehow.

'Yeah,' I replied. 'I've had a long day travelling. I'm kind of tired. If you don't mind, I'm just going to crash.' It was an understatement, but I didn't need or want them to know anything about me. They were annoying me, and I was tired and irritable. I had only just walked in the door. *God, I hope they're not on my bus.*

They started to whisper like mean girls in the playground, and I was the one they were picking on. I felt like the odd one out – they were all friends, possibly friends from high school, probably still living at home, working or going to university, maybe from a small town like my hometown.

Instantly I remembered times gone by from my youth, between the ages of nine to twelve, when I was new to my small country town school and used to be bullied in the playground. Some kids would pin all my limbs down, while another kid measured parts of my body that they thought were big. I'd never fitted into the tiny school with fewer students than a choir. Being new, I was seen as different, strange and odd. I wasn't odd. I just hadn't lived in that town my whole life.

I became quiet and shy, afraid to speak to anyone, too shy to ever say anything, about anything, to anyone in case it was the wrong thing and more bulling flew in my direction. High school was different, as I had my core group of friends. We all supported each other through the good and the bad. Sure, there were mean girls, but I didn't care about what they said, or what they did. I had gained a new level of confidence once I hit puberty. I'd learnt the hard way through junior school. Reflecting back to more recent times, it seemed I'd discovered the hard way with men too.

I had made it this far, and now I knew that I didn't need help anymore, from a teacher, friend or parent. I could stand on my own two feet; whatever they threw at me I could handle. I didn't care; I felt stronger, taller and more formidable than I ever had before.

I stood at the end of my bed and declared, 'I'm tired. I'm going to sleep. I'd appreciate it if you could keep it down, after all, it's 2 am, and I need to get up at six to leave. I'm sorry to be a party pooper, but you have no idea about the day I've had. Thanks.'

They all stood in the corner huddled together like a pack of wolves – they were either going to attack me or bow down to me – in my eyes they had no choice.

'She's right, girls, it's late. We've all got an early morning tomorrow. Let's hit the sack.'

I rolled over with my back towards them, smiling as I drifted off to sleep.

✳ ✳ ✳

The alarm clock beeped loudly; it seemed like it was directly next to my ear. I hadn't tried it out yet. And I certainly hadn't thought about what impact it would have on my fellow traveller. *Must put it under my pillow tomorrow*, I thought, as I fumbled with it to try and turn it off. I was still half asleep.

Groans were heard across the room, and then a pillow flew my way and hit the curtains, revealing a sunny sky with soft, long, streaky white clouds like an artist had just painted watercolours across the dazzling blue.

Taking a deep breath, I pushed back the covers. *This is it! This is the day. Today, I am taking the next step, on my own. I can do this.*

I could hear the shower running as I packed and waited for my turn for the bathroom.

Dressed, and after a quick check of the room, I headed out, wishing the girls all the best for their adventures, as I closed the door.

'Thank God that was only four hours of my life,' I muttered under my breath as I made my way to the lift.

Downstairs, the front doors were open and it was hot. I was still slightly unprepared for how hot London could be, and I realised that wearing jeans, t-shirt and boots were perhaps not the best choices. As I ate breakfast alone, I was happy for the time I had to collect my thoughts. I looked at the clock, 7.25 am – time to catch my next bus.

I stopped as I looked at the front door I had only just walked through hours before, and I took a long breath. My next chapter had begun.

Chapter 11

LET THE PARTY BEGIN

'Paperwork,' the redheaded lady called out to me, looking blankly into the distance as she sat behind an old, half-broken fold-out table.

Papers? What papers? I wondered. *The damn papers the travel agent did not manage to get to me? Must be.* I felt like I was in a World War II movie as a refugee trying to cross a border in Europe to escape the Nazis. I had no papers.

Staring blankly at the lady who was sitting at the table blinking while looking up at me, my heart began to race. I had nothing to hand over. *Think swiftly, Tiffany,* I said to myself. *I know, I have a passport. I'll hand them that.*

'And your travel documents?' the lady said looking at me as if I was a complete imbecile.

Apparently, I was, as I had no idea what was going on. I started moving from foot to foot. 'Ummmmm. My name is Tiffany and here is my passport – that's all I've got,' I replied nervously.

My palms started to become sweaty, with my nerves vibrating throughout my body. I hadn't thought of this. What if I couldn't get on the bus? Was I even on this trip? Had I got the day wrong? They had no record of me. What if the paperwork was so crucial that they didn't let me board this bus? *Come on, God, let me get on this tour,* I prayed, again.

'What? No papers?' she looked shocked, not quite understanding that someone could arrive without the correct documentation.

'I'm sorry, but I have no idea what you are talking about,' I said to her. 'Oh wait, I have a receipt for the trip.' I proceeded to produce the crumpled-up receipt for multiple thousands of dollars. Money in exchange for an unread map that I prayed had signposts for my life.

It took them two hours to find the so-called papers they needed, while I sat on the ground outside the bus, and everyone else sat inside the bus, glaring out the window at me, wondering what on earth was happening with the girl who didn't have her shit together – as was I.

Finally, I was able to walk up stairs of the bus and embark on my journey. The entire coach cheered in unison. *Great! Humiliated in the first five seconds of this trip, that must be a new record – so many mistakes before I even begin. It's got to get better.*

There were no obvious seats left on the bus as I walked to the end row. It looked like no one wanted me – the girl who couldn't get her shit together – to sit next to them. *Where the hell is a seat?* Everyone had a friend or a group of friends; I felt smaller than a single piece of sand in the ocean. I looked longingly for a place to hide under, like a rock, but there were no rocks on the bus – not yet anyway.

What am I doing here, I pondered, as I felt my face become redder than a beetroot.

I proceed to walk back towards the front of the bus, and there at the very front, right by the stairs was a seat. I must have missed it when I first walked on, due to my total embarrassment and humiliation. The seat now shone like a shining beacon, glowing radiantly among a sea of darkness that demons hid underneath. I slid in, giving thanks for a resting place.

Next to me sat a girl who turned to me and said, 'Don't worry, this is going to be so much fun! Hi, my name is Andrea. I bet we're going to be great friends. I'm from New Zealand, where are you from?'

Suddenly the sun started to shine. I took another deep breath and knew that everything was going to be okay. I smiled back at her.

'So, what brings you on a trip of a lifetime all on your own with no papers?' She was still smiling, so I knew that 'the sisterhood' would come to my rescue – even if I only knew one person on this jam-packed bus full of forty-nine excitable young adults who were filled with dreams and hopes of adventures.

'Well, I guess, I had to get away from my boyfriend.' *May as well just get it out there and wear my heart on my sleeve, as my heart can't get more broken than it already is.*

'Me too, what's your name?'

'Tiffany,' I replied.

'You from Oz?'

'Yep.'

'You travelling on your own then?' Andrea asked.

'Yep,' I replied, swallowing hard. 'You?'

'Nope, here with some mates from back home.' She turned around and the two guys behind us beamed at me with cheeky grins.

'Righto, it's time we got this party started,' said our leader and guide, Jo.

The bus then started up. Whoops, cheers and laughter roared out from everyone.

We were on our way.

I looked out the window, sleep deprived, humiliated, embarrassed, alone and ready to take this next step. *How hard can it be? Now I've got my new friend Andrea, I'm not alone. Yep, I can do this.*

'As everyone is getting settled, let's go through a few introductions, housekeeping and a bit of a tour of my hometown London,' Jo announced. 'First of all, my name is Jo and our trustworthy driver here is Alex. We will be sharing this journey with you, and we are here to help you, cook for you and ensure you have a great time. But first things first . . .' She proceeded with a bus version of a safety talk. We had a little hammer to knock open glass windows in case the bus crashed into the side of a mountain or fell off a cliff, plus we had a toilet and a good stereo system – what more could we possibly need?

I could hear the mumbo jumbo carrying on all around me – the ooohs and ahhs as we snaked our way through the narrow streets of London. Looking out the window, I spotted Big Ben, and then it hit me – I really was setting off on my big adventure.

My heart started to flutter. *I'm on the other side of the world. I'm here in famous places I've only ever seen on television.* It all felt familiar but surreal at the same time, like I was standing still while the rest of the world moved around me. These places really existed, and there I was looking at them, not quite knowing how to handle the strange overwhelming feelings that came across me – and then the question popped into my head. *Will I ever see this again? Oh how ridiculous, of course I will, as we have to come back to London, and I have a place to stay!*

I'd devised a plan in the early hours of the morning the night before, as I listened to the girls in my room snoring from too many beers. I had decided that I was going to work in London for a bit, and then travel to Spain, then onto Morocco and meet up with friends, and then back to London until . . . whatever happened next, I wasn't sure. But lots of travel and working sounded like a good idea to me, why wouldn't I see London again, as long as I went through with my plan.

However, the sick feeling in the pit of my stomach started to come back as I pondered my future. It was the same sick feeling I had had the night before I left home to start on this trip, when I was hiding underneath Matthew's bed. Something was telling me to take a good look around and remember this moment, as I might not get another chance.

I wondered what my intuition was trying to tell me. But instead of questioning it further, I pushed it aside – yet again.

I never knew that a clock tower could have such a profound impact on me. I'd never been a fan of Big Ben. But this, this was special; it was so significant, with so much history, so much life, I had to hold back the tears.

The West End, Piccadilly Circus, and an array of the places from a Monopoly board seemed to show up. Each one had the same overwhelming impact on me.

Leaving London, we slowly meandered through the suburbs of long, narrow lines of houses – so different from back home, with hardly any gardens and all the same colour, no vibrancy. It was all very muted and dull, a bit like the sky. No wonder people complained about an 'English Sky', it was dreary; the watercolours of early morning had disappeared. As I gazed up into the abyss of sulking grey clouds, I drifted off to sleep.

I awoke just in time before we boarded the ferry. The bus was moving, jolting almost, getting ready for us to board our next mode of transport.

'Don't leave the bus until we say so,' I heard the instructions from Jo. How on earth were we going to leave the bus if the door was closed? These doors were automatic; it wasn't like we were in a car, although maybe we could always use that little hammer . . .

It smelled like a ferry. Diesel fumes were coming up from the engine. Flashes of sea-green gentle waves came to my mind – steamy nights, seasickness and hangovers from an island far away . . . *No, I was not going to have that again. Not here and not now. I was on my journey to redemption.*

Looking out to the turquoise ocean, I could see beyond to the most incredible sight – the white cliffs of Dover. My heart beat faster. I felt engulfed by their height and strength, but their sheer size wasn't the only thing that sent me into a whirlpool of emotion. It was the sharpness of the cliffs, the way the earth had moved and formed around millions of years of erosion, yellowing in areas, creating little wriggly transverse lines that made their own patterns, telling their own story. And somehow, in all their greatness, they signified peace.

Was this sense from history lessons or from all those hours of documentaries that Dad had made me watch as a kid? Or was it something more? It felt almost like coming home and yet . . . I was nowhere near home. I wanted to run to the white sand and grab some, put it in a bottle to keep for life, like a good luck charm, but I was already on the ferry. I had no camera with me, as it was locked away in my bag on the bus. I had no opportunity to save this moment, nothing but a lasting image in my mind. I stared at the cliffs until they were specs on the horizon.

No one else seemed to feel at all like I did about being surrounded by the white cliffs of Dover. Everyone was still excited and ready for adventure, but perhaps in a different form. Some of the boys had already started drinking, while the girls stuck with their friends in their groups, all giggling, looking around nervously.

Surveying the cabin of the ferry, I had a bit more of an idea of who I would be spending the next month with. Over to my left was the 'quiet group', looking around being polite. Then there were the rowdy 'Aussie boys', joking around and being typical blokes. A few others who were travelling alone were also surveying the scene. And there were a couple of smaller groups of men and women who seemed a bit older than the rest of the group. I could hear they all had different accents, though I couldn't pick where they were from. I then noticed a group of girls who appeared friendly and smiled at me. Taking a deep breath, I walked over to them, hoping that I might finally be able to make some new friends without totally humiliating myself.

'Take a seat,' one of the girls said.

'It's quite something, ain't it,' said another girl, as we all looked out at the water.

Oh, how the sea could have told a grand story of the plethora of passengers over millennia, those who had used it as their thoroughfare. And now I was adding a verse to its great chapters – the girl from country New South Wales, Australia. I was joining its story. I was another passenger looking for a fresh breath of life. I wondered how many times the ocean had seen this story before.

Ferries, terminals, roads, cargo ships and holding bays lay before me on the edge of France as we entered our dock.

It was not quite what I was expecting, which was again another surprise.

I'd imagined rolling hills; cobblestone pathways; ladies riding bicycles with wicker baskets on the front, flowers draping over the edge with baguettes poking their way out. There were no women wearing large straw hats over long, brown hair. No ruby red lipstick to match flowing floral skirts while breathing in the fresh, clean air. There were no beaming smiles of French people waving to us on our arrival and welcoming new friends to their country.

Instead, the air was thick with smog, and there were industrial buildings as far as the eye could see. Men in old, worn clothes were sitting on boxes having smoko, yelling abuse in French at each other. The only forms of transport I saw were buses and trucks motoring down the highway that had signs and state-of-the-art lighting like something from out of space. There was not a cobblestone path in sight.

Even with the lack of historic-looking local fare and architecture, the bus was filled with ecstatic young people who were ready to take the next step on their journey – but was I?

After more housekeeping from our guide, more rules for the trip, timetables and information as we travelled towards our first stop, Paris. I drifted off into my own daydream world, not listening.

Paris . . .

The word alone oozed sophistication, romance and love. Would it live up to the city that everyone talked about? The city of love? Would I find love? I certainly wasn't looking for it. The only love I was looking for this time was self-love. Would I find it in Paris?

I hadn't even looked at the itinerary. I wasn't sure what we were doing over the next few days, or in fact throughout the trip. I was quite comfortable flying by the seat of my pants, but with all the commotion and everyone talking about what they were going to be doing, it became clear that I needed to work out what parts of the tour I would be participating in. There were a whole bunch of extra trips – some for the more adventurous, some for the tamer travellers. Jo announced that she needed to know our movements, *spoilsport*, so my intention to live on the edge dissipated in front of me.

Pulling up my daypack, I began to ruffle through the few items that I had with me. Then I found it, my white pouch with 'the paperwork', which I now had.

The options I had for Paris included a cabaret show, which sounded like fun, and a dinner – yes to that as well. *Surely all the best parts of Europe will be on this tour. So I may as well do all of them.* No need to think about anything – just be present and enjoy.

Leaning over to Jo, I said, 'Just put me down for all the extras. It's not every day you get to travel around Europe. Better make the most of it.'

There. Done. Easy. All I had to do now was participate. Not another thought had to go into what was happening next. As long as I tagged along like a little sheep, I'd be fine. I wasn't very good at being a sheep though. However, this time I'd have to try.

Chapter 12

EVERYTHING IS FABULOUS IN PARIS

The tunnels through Paris had an eerie feeling. Driving through them, everyone fell into a hush. Sadness then consumed the bus as we travelled along the motorway where only two years earlier Princess Diana had passed away due to a car accident. It was all anyone could talk about; we all looked out the dark windows into the soulless tunnels.

When we finally caught a glimpse of the Eiffel Tower, the mood lifted and the excitement was palpable. Soon our sightseeing tour had us absorbing some of France's beautifully ornate architecture – golden details on turrets, opulent columns and statues on every corner, or so it seemed. Flashes from cameras went crazy as the bus made its way through all the top tourist highlights.

I consumed every detail – the flowers of yellow and red that lined the roundabouts, people walking around with dogs leading their way, animated conversations flowing in cafés, lovers embracing each other by the Seine River, which wound its way peacefully around the city of white. I wondered what life was like for these Parisians. Were their lives like mine? Were they looking for something else in their life? Something extra?

But how could they be? They were in Paris. I was in Paris. Everything was fabulous, here in Paris. The Eiffel Tower seemed visible from almost every aspect of the city. It was magnificent.

Pulling up along the road in front of the Eiffel Tower, we were ready for the first adventurous part of the trip – going up the Eiffel Tower.

I stood under its majesty, mesmerised.

It felt impossible but possible all at the same time.

Standing in a queue among the other enthusiastic travellers, the accents from around the globe became perceptible. I could barely understand another soul in the line. Some of the girls on the tour had included me in their group in the queue. I felt a sense of relief as I joined them, squishing up beside them as we went up the elevator, daypacks clinging to our chest and smiles vast as the sky. We were here, within an icon of France, here in Paris! I felt overwhelmed.

Reaching the viewing platform, I couldn't believe how white Paris was. From up high, all you could see for miles were white buildings, mostly no more than three-storeys high. Everything looked like little white doll's houses with a pinkish hue over them as the smog rolled in. The colours of the buildings all seemed to smudge together like a Monet impressionist painting. It was no wonder everyone fell in love with Paris. I had too. There was something about the way the buildings of the city rolled into each other, moving effortlessly within its winding streets. Passion seemed to drip from every building and human being; it was impossible not to be caught up in its romance.

Arriving at our accommodation, we all scrambled out of the bus, filled with excitement and a tinge of anxiety as we looked at the timber cabins before us. They were stained in almost fluorescent orange, all lined in rows with little space between them. Grey gravel covered the narrow pathways. I was so pleased I'd brought a backpack; it was going to be hard for those with a wheelie suitcase to drag their luggage over the rough stones.

'Right everyone. You have two hours to settle yourselves. Have a drink at the bar, shower, get settled and sort out your beds before dinner. Dinner and breakfast will be served in the mess hall,' Jo announced as we were all swarming around the bags from under the bus.

The cabin I was in was to be shared with fellow passengers of smaller groups: two sisters from New Zealand, and a girl from somewhere in South America. I hadn't spoken to any of them as yet. I felt like they were staring at me as I walked into the cabin, or maybe it was just my own lack of self-worth. Perhaps I had the first-day jitters? Or was it just the fact that I had already made an impression, an impression I didn't want to make. The embarrassment was still fresh in my mind.

Throwing my bag on the bottom bunk, the air in the cabin was thick with awkwardness. I needed to get out. I excused myself and went for a walk. The campground was abuzz with excitement. Laughter, chatter, singing, sounds of sharing came from every angle. It was depressing. Finding my way to the bar, I started chatting to the bar staff, like a lonely, old person with no family and no friends sitting in their local bar drinking their life away.

The high from the day had now hit a surprising low – how quickly loneliness could sink in and suck you dry.

'I'll have another beer, please,' I said to the guy behind the bar, who could not have been much older than me. Tall, with shaggy blond hair, he had that backpacker/adventurer look about him – leather necklace and t-shirt with holes all through it. Evidently, he spent his money on a good time rather than clothes.

I turned to walk away when Andrea came up to me. 'There you are,' she said. 'I've been searching all over for you. I've got stuck in a cabin with people I don't know yet; let's stick together and stay in the same room at the next stop.'

I beamed. Maybe I had made a friend.

'Sounds good,' I said enthusiastically.

'Oh, you've already got a beer, good; come on, I'm getting one too.'

The rest of our group slowly started to make their way over to the bar and finally into the mess hall for a BBQ dinner.

'Dinner will be served soon,' Jo announced. 'But first, we try snails!'

The thought of eating a snail repulsed most of the group. There were screams of disgust, with faces being pulled in every contortion. I giggled watching everyone. All the extroverted people made a big song and dance about trying a snail, while the quiet ones merely looked on, continuing to pull faces. I ate the snail happily, regardless of what everyone else thought. It was buttery, with a strong garlic flavour, silky in texture with earthy undertones. I quite liked it.

The following day we were free to do whatever we liked – see museums or check out a few more sites – it was entirely up to us, as long as we were back for dinner at a Parisian restaurant and then onto the cabaret show.

I couldn't wait. What would I do with this freedom?

Andrea caught me over breakfast. 'So . . .' she said while eating yoghurt and cereal, and sipping on orange juice. 'What do you want to do today?'

'Hmm . . . I'm not sure. I don't think I want to go and see a whole bunch of museums. I think I'd rather soak up the daily life of being a Parisian. Drink coffee – well a cup of tea for me – in a café and eat croissants. Live like a local.'

'Sounds perfect,' replied Andrea.

Smiling at each other, we made loose plans for the day.

A group of us all had the same idea. We made our way to the Arc de Triomphe. We were in awe of its presence and terrified by the traffic, which didn't stop us from wondering aimlessly down the Champs-Elysées. Finding cheese and wine, we placed ourselves in a park underneath trees. Eating and drinking, we watched the world go by, losing ourselves in the beauty of Paris.

Our day was filled with an abundance of French life – eating macarons, drinking Perrier under the blistering sun while sitting on the sidewalk in a café – it was far too hot for tea. Meandering along the Seine, we watched lovers swoon by the river and artists creating their master-pieces. And all the while I was making friends. Sharing our experiences made it even more joyous.

I was going to be alright. I was going to have a group of friends on this trip. Maybe, they would be friends for life. But for now, to have the company of others was all I needed.

Our tummies and hearts were full by the time we made our way back to the campsite. We were enjoying life after a couple of beers, and it was time to get ready for our next move – a night out on the town.

Showering and getting dressed in my grey top; short, black skirt and strappy shoes, I was ready for the evening's events. I had my hair done, signature dark eye make-up of black eyeliner, black eye shadow with silver highlights to bring out the blue in my eyes, and a nude lip gloss. The girls staying in my cabin looked at me up and down, eyes wide – I knew I looked hot and sexy. I was in Paris, how else was I going to dress?

Grabbing my leather jacket and throwing it over my shoulder, I called out to them as I stepped out of our cabin, 'Don't wait up, girls.' And I winked at them. That would get them talking. At least my reputation might move on from 'the girl who couldn't get her shit together' to 'the foxy lady'.

Dinner was upstairs in a little restaurant that was down a side street of Paris. The staircase creaked and moaned as we made our way single file to where our meal was to be served. Music flowed from the room we were headed towards, and a Frenchman with a big, round face greeted us as he played a giant piano accordion strapped to his body. *This is going to be fun.*

French champagne was poured, and an exquisite three-course meal started with a Nicoise salad, and for main we had Duck à l'Orange, and then crème caramel for dessert. The wine flowed, French music played, and we all sang along making up the words in our best faux-French.

Stumbling down the stairs and heading out into the warm night air, I began to realise that perhaps I had had one too many drinks, even though I had promised myself I would not partake in such activities. I had got lost in the moment, again, with the music, the chatting and the fun of it all. It was a bad habit of mine, only now I was in a foreign country, and I hardly knew a soul. I needed to be respectful – respectful of my new surrounds, of myself, and my country. Andrea and I began walking through the streets of Paris, arm in arm, singing songs as we made our way to the cabaret show.

Entering the Montmartre district with its notorious nightlife, the building we went into gave me the sense that I was stepping back in time into a 1920s speakeasy. On the ground floor, there were tables for two with Art Deco lamps randomly placed. The stalls above contained seats in a theatre style. The Art Deco theme continued with lamps lining the walls, giving the hall a warm glow. Waiters in tuxedos wondered around offering guests champagne, with a bar situated at the back of the hall. The stage was set with a giant, red, velvet curtain, closed, waiting to be opened to unveil the colour and excitement of the can-can dancers, possibly the best dancers in the world.

Andrea gestured for me to grab a table and that she was going to get us a drink.

The chair dragged making a loud sound as I pulled it out from the table and slumped into it. *God I hope she gets me a bottle of water.* I tried to grab her attention but it was no use, people were coming through the door thick and fast. I didn't dare leave our table; there was now only standing room.

Andrea came back with a bottle of champagne and two glasses, no water.

'It was awful getting back here,' she said, pouring us both a glass of champagne.

'Where did all these people come from?'

I looked at her, and then at the champagne – there was no way we were going to be able to get back to the bar without missing the show. I was stuck, with champagne and no water.

'When in France . . .' Andrea said raising her glass.

'Do as the French do,' I ended her sentence as we clinked our glasses and then sipped on our champagne.

The lights went dim and the air became stuffy; the crowd moved closer to the stage.

Andrea topped up our glasses.

The music began playing the infamous can-can music Offenbach, and the crowd cheered and clapped.

The show was hypnotic with its colourful skirts and incredibly high kicks; they were the most flexible dancers I had ever seen. I could see why they were so risqué in their day – there were a lot of legs, frills and knickers showing.

Making our way out into the night after the show, we passed bars and shops still thriving with life.

The bars looked so inviting – French music playing, cute French guys sitting at bars smiling at us as we lingered a little too long outside the windows. We decided to go in, just for one more drink. Why not? We were in Paris; it was our last night there. Plus, we had the address of our accommodation if we got lost.

More champagne, more music, more dancing, it wasn't until the early hours of the morning that we decided it was time to head back to our accommodation. Hollering for a taxi as we stumbled by the side of the road, we found out accommodation note and handed it to the driver. It seemed to take forever; we were sure he was taking us the long way to make more money out of us. I didn't care though. I just need to get back to my cabin and into bed. We were exhausted and very, very drunk.

We made it back safely to the campsite. The gravel beneath our feet crunched loudly, as we entered in the password into the security system for the gate, letting ourselves in like kids sneaking back into the house past curfew. The campsite was mostly silent, except for a dull noise coming from the bar.

'I'm beat,' Andrea said, hugging me. 'See you in a few hours.' She giggled and made her way back to her cabin.

I couldn't bear waking up the girls in my cabin, so I went towards the noise of the bar. There were only a few people left by now. I pulled up a chair and asked for a Coke and a beer.

The next thing I recall was the sun shining in on me. I was alive, but where was I? I quickly surveyed my surrounds with one eye open.

Why did I have more drinks on top of drinks? I am never going to 'find myself' within a stranger's sheets.

Rolling over, I saw the back of a naked man with scruffy blond hair.

Shit. The staff member from the bar. Shit. Shit. Shit.

Slowly I crept around the room gathering my things and made a quick exit. God, what time was it? The campsite was a hive of activity; people were moving about with bags, calling out to their friends, running around.

Had I missed the bus?

Opening the door to my room, all my cabin mates looked at me in horror as I entered the room in last night's clothes. My bunk was a complete mess, just how I'd left it. All their gear was all packed up, and they were showered, dressed and probably fed, and I assumed that they didn't have the hangover I had.

Head down, I quietly walked over to where the volcano of Tiffany's belongings lay and searched for my clock.

7.55 am.

'SHIT!' I said out loud.

The bus left at 8 am. I had five minutes to get my gear together and get on the bus. I quickly stripped out of last night's clothes and put on whatever I saw first. Then I shoved everything into my bag as fast as

I could. Praying I hadn't left anything behind, I ran out of the room and headed towards the bus like I was running for my life. Passing the mess hall, I raced in and swiftly grabbed a bottle of water to help this Godforsaken hangover, skidding in the gravel at the bus as Jo looked at me when ticking off the names.

'You just made it, again,' she said, looking at me with uncertainty. 'Alex, open the hatch back up please, we have a dawdler.'

Sheepishly, I grinned at Alex as he opened the hatch. 'Thanks,' I said. 'No problem.'

Walking on the bus . . . late . . . again . . . everyone glared at me, and then the whispers started. *Great, just great! I'm making a name for myself. I've gone back to 'can't get her shit together' girl, but maybe now, it's 'can't get her shit together, parties too hard' girl. That was a step up at least.*

Sliding in beside Andrea, who'd saved me a seat this time, I looked at her with relief. 'Looks like you got up to more fun than me last night,' she said winking.

The bus engine started up its vibrational hum, something I would come to appreciate, and then Jo's voice came on the speakerphone, as it would every time we got on the bus. A warm greeting was announced followed by an outline of the day ahead, filling us all with enthusiasm – which was never hard.

'Good morning, everyone! Every morning when we depart our destination, this is the first thing you will hear once you are on the bus. It is our tour group song. Sit back, relax and enjoy,' Jo pressed play. *You only get what you give* by the New Radicals then blasted out of the stereo. We would hear it every day for the next twenty days.

Taking a long gulp of water, I visualised myself coming onto the bus, inconspicuously, just like everyone else, with no one looking at me or judging me, which was unlike how it felt in that moment. And what made it worse was that I'd brought it on myself. Damn it, why had I consumed so much champagne and God knows what else? I wished the bus was stowing me away to somewhere peaceful, with no one snickering at me behind my back and with no alcohol consumption. Or maybe I could just be swallowed up whole.

No such luck. The bus continued to murmur and snicker.

'Don't worry,' Andrea said. 'It will be someone else's turn tomorrow.'

Taking a deep breath, I closed my eyes and waited for the embarrassment to pass.

Chapter 13

NEW FRIENDS

I was no longer the centre of attention with everyone talking about me; everyone had moved on, looking at the scenery and getting ready for our next destination. I was now old news. My wishes had been fulfilled, although I wasn't in a truly peaceful place. People started to go into their own worlds as we travelled long distances. The opportunity for a nap plus the gentle rocking of the bus sent most of the passengers to sleep, or at least into a peaceful lull.

I was hungry. In fact, I was starving. The sun was streaming in through the windows of the bus; I had little to shade me. I hadn't thought about what I would need while sitting on the bus, waiting to get to our next destination. I didn't have a book anymore and now I had run out of water. I was hot and hungry and tired, and we'd only been on the bus for an hour.

Jo spoke into her microphone again. I'd stopped listening. My head hurt and I was getting grumpier by the second.

'There is a café over to your left for those of you who are hungry.'

My ears pricked up. *Food. Hurray!*

'You are welcome to wander around for the next hour on your own. Be sure to be back on the bus by ten o'clock.'

Grabbing my bag, I raced out of the bus and headed straight for the café, getting rocks in my sandals as I ran. It appeared that everyone had the same idea, as when I turned around, the line seemed to have become incredibly long all of a sudden.

'J'voudrais un baguette au fromage et jambon s'il vous plait,' I asked the lady behind the counter with an enormous smile on my face. I couldn't believe how much high-school French had just come back to my mind. A surge of self-confidence washed over me. 'Et une du jus d'orange.'

The lady behind the counter smiled at me and replied in French.

And I understood every word. I felt a buzz within as I looked back at everyone waiting in the line. I proudly held my freshly purchased French food, ordered in French in France. *Who cares what everyone thinks about me? I can speak French!*

Soaking up the Mediterranean sun, my mood took a 180-degree turn while I munched down on my delicious sandwich as if it was the first meal I had ever had. My heart began to sing as my tummy started to fill. It was like I had discovered a tiny puzzle piece to my soul.

Not far from Lyon, our next stop was Theize – a village in the wine region of Beaujolais, famous for its red wines. I hated red wine, a bit like hating coffee, though maybe it was time to give red wine another try? While in France, do as the French do, right? It appeared that living like a local was my motto for the trip, and as such, I would continue to do so.

Green rolling hills were covered by ribbed lines of grapevines spanning out across farmland for as far as the eye could see. The bright blue sky was almost iridescent as it moved across the horizon, and fluffy white clouds were scattered above the vines. Another picture postcard stood before me.

Our accommodation, Chateau De Cruix, sat right in among the vines and rolling hills. A terrace wrapped itself around the chateau on the ground floor leading to a butterfly staircase that framed the front of the chateau and led out onto a rolling green lawn. Deck chairs were randomly placed for rest and relaxation for guests while looking out onto the pool. The chateau was three-storeys high, with a wing that spanned two-storeys to the east. It sat prominently overlooking vineyards. Farmhouses made of stone and brick with red-tiled roofs popped up randomly in the distance.

The sixteenth-century chateau was typical Lyon renaissance-style architecture. It was grand in design, constructed of stone, with blue serpentine tiles lining the roundel roofs on every corner, towering over the property. Quoin corners lined its boundaries, and there were double French windows that opened on every floor, allowing the breeze to blow the sweet scent of summer through the corridors.

It seemed that all of France, the United Kingdom, and no doubt many parts of the rest of Europe would have incredible old buildings filled with histories and stories, if only the walls could speak.

It was hot in France. Some of the boys jumped in the pool and instantly jumped out like squealing monkeys – the water was still icy cold. Everyone laughed as they watched on, still hot, but now not game enough to try out the pool.

Settling into the chateau, we found ourselves grabbing a French-style basket, a bottle of local Beaujolais red wine, a baguette, cheese, ham and some fruit. The whole tour group wandered off into the sun for an afternoon of merriment in the country. Locals called out 'Bonjour' as we walked by. This was more like what I had imagined France to be like. Warm and welcoming, with kind, cheerful characters filling the streets.

We came to the top of a hill that we only just managed to climb. We were all hot and bothered and thirsty. Not a spec of shade was in sight, but what a glorious view. A patchwork blanket of farmland decorated with vines covered the rolling hills, with little farmhouses sitting up straight and tall alongside them. Everyone was relaxed and happy as we spent the hours of the day daydreaming about our lives – and everyone talked about where they had been and what their lives were like back home.

I fell silent. I didn't want to think about my recent past. I didn't want to recall any of it – not the darkness within myself I was still so desperately trying to forget. That part of me, I wasn't prepared to share yet.

Making a swift exit, I headed back to the chateau, alone.

The heat rose over the next few days. Everyone continued to be hot and bothered. Our next destination was further south, to Barcelona, Spain.

Rattle . . . bang . . . snap.

The bus suddenly stopped. Our bathroom on the bus no longer worked – if you needed a toilet stop, you had to go when we stopped. On announcement of this news, the groans were louder than a waterfall. Alex got out and did some bus-maintenance magic and we were on the road again, though the relaxing hum of the bus now played a different tune – one which sounded more like a high-pitched, buzzing rattle.

Heading over the border into Spain, we were held up for a while at border protection. All of us were told to keep a low profile and wait, passports in hand. The energy on the bus was of nerves and filled with tension.

Travelling safely across the border, Jo announced that a new bus would be arriving for us soon, which would hopefully be in Barcelona, but possibly the south of France. They weren't sure when or where, but it would be soon.

We made it to Barcelona and checked out the sights like we did in the other cities – it seemed to be the theme for the tour – we moved throughout the city and ended back at a familiar sight, a cabin site, just like the one in Paris. The other tour group had already arrived and taken up all the good cabins. I'd seen these guys before, back in Paris. We would cross over with them throughout our adventures as we zigzagged our way around Europe, sharing cabin sites along the way.

The sangria flowed with ease, while we got ready for our Spanish fiesta. I made my way over to the bar, making a few more new friends. I was beginning to like getting to know everyone, the fear and isolation of the last two years with Patrick was slowly starting to dissolve within my soul. Sangria after sangria, paella and more sangria, we all ended up dancing and singing and making a lot of noise.

My new friends were great, but loneliness began to rear its ugly head inside me again. I longed to be held, longed to be loved, by someone, anyone. Love, I missed love.

The air was thick, hot and sticky, just like being back in the tropics of Queensland. The humidity was higher than France or England. I guessed we were a lot further south. The trip so far had been exhausting – possibly due to burning the candle at both ends – making the most out of every moment we had. Finally, we had had a day off to do as we liked, without anyone telling us what to do, just like our day off in Paris. It was a pleasure. There was, of course, the option of doing all the touristy things, but I for one wanted nothing more than to lie by the pool, get a suntan and drink sangria. Another day of escaping through alcohol – maybe the loneliness would evaporate out of my system.

I watched our group pile back on the bus, daypacks on, cameras around their necks – we really did look like a bunch of tourists. Oh well, that's what we were.

Bikini on, towel in hand, I headed straight for the pool. As I set up my spot for the day, one of the other girls from my tour, Fie, walked in behind me.

'Hey, looks like we've got the same idea,' she said smiling at me. 'Mind if I join you?'

'Sure thing,' I replied, excitement building in me with the possibility of another new friend.

We lay in the sun, giggling and discussing the adventures we had had so far and how magnificent the Spanish sun was on our very white bodies.

'I think it's time to go shopping!' I declared. 'Maybe we can catch up tonight for a drink before we head into town for the Spanish feast!'

The Mediterranean sun had filled me with new-found confidence and self-esteem long forgotten, like an old sparkplug being replaced. I was determined to do something with it – prove to myself that I could!

'Sounds like a plan,' replied Fiona, my new-found friend.

With a map in my hand, and sunglasses on, I delicately made my way out of the safety zone of our tour campsite and out into the unknown streets of Barcelona.

Hopping on a bus and praying to God that I had got onto the right one, I headed straight to the city. This bus was different from the other buses I had been catching over the last few months. It was filled to the brim with locals, and I knew no Spanish at all. A diverse collection of the community sat hunched over vinyl seats with their families all huddled in close to each other.

There were men with no teeth and thick, greasy, black hair, and men with smart business suits on, styled to perfection. It was everyone and anyone on the bus; I was in the thick of it all and loving it. It felt like everyone was staring at me, the fish out of water, but I didn't care. I smiled at those staring and looked down at my daypack resting against my chest and held onto it just a little bit tighter.

The city was filled with old and new, with modern towering buildings populating parts of the radiant blue skyline sticking out like fresh flowers emerging from the winter snow. Lower down were older buildings that carried the same historical sense as other buildings across Europe. Cobblestone pathways mixed in with modern concrete walkways all intertwined and blended like the vines of bramble bushes.

Moving my way among the crowds, I saw masses of women going in the direction of an enormous staircase that reached up towards a huge sign. I figured the sign read 'SALE', though I knew no Spanish to save myself, but I knew a sale sign when I saw one. If my shopping radar was right, it looked to me that there was a significant sale on.

I watched the women walking down the staircase in the highest of high heels I had ever seen. They managed to walk down like they were on the catwalk. Their long, gorgeous dark hair was flowing, and they were wearing tight-fitting clothes that showed off their best assets – legs, butts, chests – it was all on display for the world to admire while they carried copious bags of items. Every woman coming down towards me looked incredible and oozed sex appeal.

Entering the building surrounded by people, mostly women, and rows and rows and rows of clothes, I wondered where to begin. Voices boomed, excitement rose as the prospect of finding something 'just for you' grew. Trying to make my way through the crowd, I kept getting shoved and pushed, and wasn't even able to get inside. I was barged at every angle. It was like Boxing Day sales on steroids.

Well, when in Spain, do as the Spanish do.

I started pushing a bit, which felt rude. I kept apologising to everyone as I tried to make my way towards a clothing rack. Some people just looked on at me as if I was a complete idiot, and still I couldn't get near the clothing rack.

Right, time to play little miss bossy!

I moved with a little more force and people started to get out of my way without a fuss. I was like a boat gliding through the water smashing against the waves. Somehow it worked among the mayhem. I came to a rack of clothes that looked to be about my size. Like a ray of sunshine sent from heaven, a fluorescent pink dress jumped out at me. It had turquoise and yellow flowers on it, with green stems all along the bottom, almost like a garden. It was made out of some crinkly type of material and was perfect for this heat!

Grabbing the hanger before anyone else did, I held it up against myself. It hung like a wet rag against my body, but stretching it out, it would show all my curves in all the right places, just like the women walking down the stairs. It was bold; it was sexy; it was the one!

That was quick! Reaching up on my tippy toes, I looked around to see where I should head next. I spotted shoes and handbags. *Perfect!* I made a beeline towards them, ready to find my next item.

A pair of black wedges with grey straps crisscrossing their way across the tops of my feet stood out among the piles of shoes. I slid them on. Comfort called out to me; they fit like a glove. I had to have them. Perfect for night wear or day wear. But there wasn't an appropriate handbag in sight.

I had wanted to become one of the women walking down the enormous staircase with bags of items, and now, there I was . . . I was doing my best to be just like them, look just like them, walk just like them and have that same air of self-confidence that I once had. And thankfully, in my post-glow spend, I could feel confidence licking at my fingertips. It's called 'retail therapy' for a reason!

* * *

Giant paellas arrived on our tables in the restaurant for our Spanish feast. The paella pans were almost as large as the table. The smell of fresh seafood and spices drifted through the air. As the night moved on, so did our volume, going up decibel by decibel. It was time to move on. A few of us decided to make our way to a nightclub and check out the nightlife in Barcelona.

A waterway ran along the front of the building with giant chains linking the pathway. People were all around, drinking and laughing. Music played from every corner. The staircase to the nightclub was lit up bright blue; the club was empty with only a few people dancing.

'I love this song,' one of the girls from the tour group screamed, grabbing her friend's hands and running towards the dance floor, now filling it just a fraction more.

I just stood there alone. I had hoped that the adventures so far would have ignited a connection with someone – anyone – forming friendships that I longed to hold in the palm of my hand. However, those I had connected with were nowhere to be seen, and I still wasn't sure I could really trust them.

The hollowness I felt within me was growing at a rapid rate. The high from my shopping trip had plummeted to an all-time low, gone like a Genie in a bottle – poof! That's the problem with retail therapy, it only lasts for such a short period of time. I headed to the bar to contemplate my sorrows and drown them out – as I had done some many times before.

Grabbing a stool and plonking myself down, I put my face in my hands.

What am I doing here, I thought for the one-thousandth time this trip.

'Why the glum face?' said a voice next to me.

I recognised it. Looking up, I couldn't believe my eyes; it was one of the guys from the resort in Queensland, one of the chefs.

We looked at each other in total disbelief.

'What are you doing here?' we said at precisely the same time, reaching over and embracing each other.

Suddenly, my loneliness vanished. A connection. I now had someone from my previous life to fill the engulfing void that echoed through my heart.

We chatted for what felt like hours. He told me how he had left the resort and started working in London, and how he was in Barcelona just for a few days. He then planned to travel around Europe a bit before going back home to Australia to make some money and then start up his own restaurant. The restaurant he worked for in London was always looking for staff, he told me. I would easily be able to get a job there, and he would be my reference – *how fantastic!* I could get a job with him at his own restaurant one day too, maybe as the restaurant manager. *Even better!* Now I had a place to stay and a job in London, and maybe even back home. Everything was falling into place. We exchanged phone numbers and promised to be in touch on my return to London.

I felt lighter within myself; my sense of feeling lost subsided slightly. Grabbing another drink, I joined my new friends on the dance floor.

However, my many celebratory drinks with my long-lost friend came undone as I found myself becoming jealous of others and their connections. My mind went into a spin, fuelled by the alcohol, and it filled with my own self-doubt. *Why can't I have a good, true, honest friendship with someone? Someone I can really be 'me' with?*

Panic set in, which soon turned to fear, which turned into hatred for those around me, for they were loved. I was not loved by anyone there. I desperately longed to be loved again. I hurled my drink at unsuspecting revellers on the dance floor and ran off into the ladies toilets, locking myself in and sobbing my heart out. The pain and the suffering from all the years with Patrick began playing out in my mind.

I was angry and the alcohol was a burning fire within my soul.

'Tiff? You okay?' Andrea asked outside the toilet door.

Slumped on the ground, unable to speak or move, I lay there in my shallow puddle of self-pity. I'd made a fool of myself again. Yet there was Andrea, caring for me, acknowledging me, being there for me – being a friend.

I had totally overreacted.

'Can you hear me, Tiff?'

'I think she's passed out,' Andrea said to someone else.

I wallowed in self-hatred on the floor.

'Maybe we should crawl under the door and check on her?'

It was Fiona.

'I'm the smallest; I'll look under the door,' came another voice. It was Sasha, another one of Fiona's friends.

My eyes were still closed, and I was unable to move, with too much alcohol and emotional pain engulfing me. I stayed on the floor.

As a face peaked underneath the door, I opened my eyes.

'Hey honey, you okay?' came the familiar voice.

Nodding, but not moving, tears flowed down my face.

'How about you open the door and we can all get out of this stinky toilet?'

Nodding again, I got up, holding onto the wall, and then reaching forward, I vomited violently into the toilet.

'I'm sorry,' I mumbled as I flushed away the hurt and pain that came out of me, and then I opened the door.

Andrea flew her arms around me. 'Come on, you. I think we've had enough excitement for one night, don't you think?'

Nodding again, I grabbed hold of her as we walked out the door.

Sasha passed me some water, winking at me. 'It's okay. We've all made mistakes before,' she said.

'Oh no, they're all looking,' said Fiona as we left the safety of the toilet.

Quickly, Andrea, Sasha and Fiona huddled around me to protect me – and to stop me from falling over – as everyone stared at us walking out of the nightclub.

They got me home quickly and tucked me into bed. I was asleep before I could even say thank you.

* * *

Head pounding, my eyes opened to blistering bright light. I saw everyone packing for our next leg of the trip. Terrified that I had ruined any chance of friendship with my fellow travellers, I sheepishly walked into the mess hall for an orange juice and a piece of toast, something to settle my stomach. I found Andrea, Fiona and Sasha eating breakfast together; they greeted me with enormous smiles that lit up the entire mess hall. A flood of relief fell over me; it looked like I hadn't ruined any potential friendships.

Sitting down, I thanked them for coming to my rescue. They didn't know how much it meant to me that they had all cared about me as a friend, a real friend, especially after my behaviour. I told myself that I needed to calm down and stop letting alcohol bring up all of my emotions that I was otherwise quite happy to hide.

Discussions of what was next, plans, ideas and expectations all floated across the room among the sniggers and looks that were directed at me. Andrea patted my knee and smiled.

With a little more love coming towards me, filling my soul, I was able to keep my head high.

Next stop, Nice. This time, it would be different, I promised myself.

Chapter 14

SLOWLY MOVING FORWARD

Getting on the bus later that day, the heat in my face from my own humiliation seemed to linger down into my neck for a little longer than expected. Too scared to look anyone in the eye, I chose sleep, again, as I still felt it safer to avoid anyone.

Then suddenly there was a jerk, and the bus crashed and banged and then came to an abrupt halt. Steam hissed from the undercarriage. Our already broken bus had now broken down, again.

'What's happened?' I groggily asked Andrea.

'Don't know.'

'Alright, everyone, settle down,' Jo called out in an attempt to calm the troops. 'Alex is going to take a look outside and see what's going on. We'll keep you posted. NO ONE is to leave the bus!' Her voice changed from calming to authoritative in that one sentence.

Groans sounded in every direction.

'I wonder where we are?' I asked Andrea, looking out the window.

Miles and miles of sunflowers surrounded us, shining their happy faces up towards the light; the sight was magnificent. Although I was disappointed that the bus had broken down, I was glad I'd been woken up to see such a glorious sight.

Fiona, who was sitting behind me, leaned over the top of the seat. 'No one knows,' she said, looking at me and ruffling my hair. 'How's your head?'

Groaning, I looked up at her and grimaced.

'Have some more water; you'll be right,' she said before sinking back down into her chair.

Everyone on the bus was getting restless; people started moving seats and making more noise. Alex and Jo consulted outside the bus as they tried to work out a plan for what was next.

Jo stepped wearily onto the stairs on the bus; she seemed tired. 'Looks like the engine has overheated. We're going to wait a while till it cools down and then see if we can get going. Once we are in Nice, head office will send us another bus. So for now, chill out, we could be here a while.'

'But Jo, JO, JO, JOOOOO . . .' people started calling out. It was like a scene from a press conference in the White House when the president stops taking questions and journalists start pounding him with questions. Jo walked back off the bus.

We were stuck there – no air-conditioning, no food or water, other than what we had all brought, and still no toilet. Hopefully, it wasn't going to take too long.

It seemed like hours that we had been sitting on the bus, overheating, hungry and over it! Anytime Jo made her way onto the bus, everyone bombarded her. 'Please let us off the bus!' The temperature was rising – the bus was like an oven. Jo hopped on and off and on and off many times, looking worried.

'Rule number one as a tourist guide is to always keep the passengers safe,' Jo announced. 'And rule number two is to always keep the passengers on the bus. In this instance, however, I think it's better that you don't die of heat exhaustion on the bus, so rule one overrides rule two. Everyone off the bus.'

Sighs of relief filled every available space within the cabin. Everyone filed out, moving to the side of the road and taking a seat in the gutter. Others were surveying the landscape to see if there was any possible way they could do a bush wee. Unfortunately, there were no hidden places. We were in full sight of the entire highway, though some didn't care.

* * *

Hours later, after sitting in the blistering sun surrounded by the sunflowers and watching them move with the sun, our next bus arrived. Cheers from the crowd echoed over the sunflowers.

We eventually made it to Nice, but I couldn't help wondering if this was only by chance.

Our cabins were made of wood, same as the others, but these ones were tinted a darker brown, not the hideous orange colour we had seen previously.

Andrea and I, plus Kimberly and Tanya, two other girls travelling alone, all bunked in together. It worked out best for everyone if we shared a room; this way everyone else could stay with their travel companions. I had now come to realise that I was not the only person on tour travelling alone, there were a few of us, and we were all perfectly happy to be sharing our cabin and our journey together.

After my antics over the past week or so, which had not been my best moments at all, I had created a bond, a trust and a love with the other young women who I now called my friends. I started to feel connected to them, though I still felt a pang of uncertainty as I found it difficult to trust, even in a friendship. All the small-town ways I had grown up with and the hurt from Patrick had really taken a toll on my ability to trust others. However, I knew time would tell if I could really trust them or not. My heart seemed to have a wall around it; I was scared to pull it down too much or let anyone in too close.

The heat continued to rise. Nice was as hot as Barcelona. Rifling through my bag, I realised I desperately needed to wash my clothes – they were nothing short of revolting. All I had left clean were my jeans and a t-shirt. My bathers stunk as they hadn't dried properly from Spain and seemed to soak their stink into every other part of my bag. Dumping every single item of my worldly possessions onto my bottom bunk, I emptied out my bag and aired it out, opening it up like a crocodile mouth – it almost appeared endless inside. Kimberly looked on at me giggling; she too had the same problem – although she was smart and had put her bathers in a plastic bag, another thing I had not been prepared for.

There was a tiny window at the back of our cabin that faced south – towards the sun. We all placed our bags on the top bunk under the open window. Together we washed and laundered our clothes like washerwomen in a village. The few of us that were left hanging around the campsite then decided it was time for exploring; the others had taken the tourist option and headed out early that morning.

Enjoying my 'live like a local' concept so much, some of us decided to keep the movement going – live like a local again and head to the train station.

Achieving success again in French, I purchased a ticket for us to head to Cannes. I had become a go-to person for assistance with French, and while I didn't know as much as one of the other girls who spoke fluent French, I could help out a bit. It was another notch up in my self-confidence.

The train was old, like one of the Sydney trains we used to catch into the city when we were kids. Burgundy red on the outside, it was battered and bruised from too many hours running along the tracks. Windows were opened to let in the breeze and sticky green vinyl seats were squashed in together. There was no air-conditioning, of course. We all climbed aboard; it felt like the train took a long, deep breath in while it waited.

Slowing moving forward, the sound of the train was unfamiliar to the hum of the bus. A change in transport was welcomed. Everyone discussed the opportunities of the day and if by chance they would see a famous movie star. I started to daydream again, a habit I had lost in my years with Patrick. But now that I was no longer under his control, I enjoyed the warmth of my imagination flourishing again.

Looking out to the sea, I thought of past wars. How much blood had been shed there? Was this train line in operation during the World Wars? Who had perished? Who had survived? Were soldiers able to work through the bounty that the sea provided or was it filled with bloodstains and warships on the horizon? I shuddered at the thought, bringing myself back to the now.

The sea was beautiful as it sparkled underneath the Mediterranean sun. But I still thought the Pacific Ocean was hard to beat.

Breaks squealing, engine crunching, the train stopped. We were at Cannes, and it was getting hotter. Dispersing, we made our own way to different destinations.

A few of us stuck together, including Fiona, Sasha and the two other friends they were travelling with. Wondering the streets of Cannes was like walking around Rodeo Drive. Blue and white bell awnings hovered above shop entry doors. Lamborghinis, Ferraris, Austin Martins were all parked on the side of the street. Women were wearing oversized sunglasses, with tight-fitting dresses and stilettos on, and they all had tiny handbags hanging over their arms. Chihuahuas poked their heads out the top of some, growling at passers-by.

With our daypacks on, our hair in ponytails, some of us with baseball caps, and wearing jeans and shorts, we could not have looked more out of place. I didn't dare go into a bar; I was sure they wouldn't let us in.

After hours of people watching and wandering aimlessly, I ventured off on my own. Catching the train back to Nice, I decided to have a look around. The town was much more down-to-earth than Cannes. I didn't feel nearly as out of place. The temperature was still rising by the second. Heading for an ice-cream van by the side of the cobblestone pathway, I saw they had my favourite flavour – pistachio.

One lick of the ice cream and I was taken to new heights of deliciousness! The coolness of the ice cream inside my stifling hot body was a relief. Savouring every mouthful, I licked the ice-cream fast as it ran down my arms. I felt nothing but pure pleasure right in that moment. It's funny how food can do that to you.

The seaside was across the road from me. I could hear it calling my name; the sound of the waves crashing against the stones filled me with an overwhelming urge to go swimming. I couldn't take the heat any longer. I thought that I might explode from being so hot, either that or pass out.

I found a spot among the stones – no sand – and buried my belongings; it was the only thing I could think of as I had my passport with me and I didn't want it to get wet or ruined, nor did I want it stolen.

Satisfied with my burying technique, I stripped off down to my bra and knickers and ran into the water like a toddler running into the sea, jumping and frolicking in the waves. The coolness covered every inch of my body; I felt the steam coming off the top of my head. With the relief from the heat, I didn't care that all I had on was my underwear; I was too hot to care! And anyway, it looked like a bikini – sort of. I would never see any of the people ever again and all I felt was pure bliss in that moment.

Lying on the hot stones felt somewhat different to the soft, golden sand on the beach in Australia, but I was happy to notice that not one single person had looked offended at my underwear or my crazy dash for a swim. *Must be a French thing.*

The water cooled me in the blistering midday sun as it seared my skin. And in a very un-Australian way, I burnt my skin to a crisp. When I was dry enough to get dressed again, I grabbed my things and headed back to camp. I could feel my skin starting to stretch, so I lathered on the moisturiser, knowing that I was in trouble. It had only been a few hours since my trip to the beach, and already I was showing up pink. Oh well, I didn't care. I'd been swimming in the French Riviera – in my knickers!

That night was our Monte Carlo casino night – time for my new dress from Barcelona. It was everything I had hoped for. It clung in places I wanted it to, but it was cool and loose and oh so comfortable, especially with so much sunburn covering my body. I was now red from head to toe and starting to feel nauseated. I clearly had sunstroke.

Drinking gallons of water and taking some paracetamol, I refused to miss out on the night. I never knew when I would get the opportunity to go again. I didn't look the 'hot, sexy Aussie' girl this time, more like the 'international traveller who didn't know when to put sunscreen on' girl. With my red skin, new dress, a thumping headache and upset tummy, I joined our group, only to notice that I wasn't alone in the sunburn stakes. *Yes! This time it isn't just me!*

Outside the casino, red Ferrari's were parked around the roundabout entrance – a much more glamorous way to arrive than in our new bus, which had been replaced that day. I say 'new' because it was new to us; however, it was very, very old, and still had no working toilet.

I thought of William as I entered the casino, longing to share the moment with him and his driving cap and his kind eyes. He would have loved looking on at all the beautiful automobiles and playing the tables. *I must tell him about this night when I get back to England.*

The casino we entered was all white, with ornate Corinthian columns lining the entrance to a veranda that was two storeys high. Colossal mahogany double doors opened out to a red velvet-roped walkway with security guards dressed in fitted black suits standing guard by the doors.

We walked straight in.

Roulette tables, baccarat and black jack were in the room, surrounded by handsome men in Armani suits and beautiful women in their slinky dresses.

I have never been a big gambler, and I'm still not, but . . . when in Monte Carlo, live like the locals, so grabbing Andrea I put some money down on roulette. I had no idea how to play, but Andrea had played it before and at least knew the rules.

Sitting on the stool, I looked around me. One player was an older man with grey thinning hair and glasses, his face hollow and eyes like glass staring at the table as it went around. Two other women who sat on the other side of me were roughly my age; both of them wore cocktail dresses ready for a night out.

I won just enough money to buy Andrea and I a round of drinks. Making our way to the bar, I couldn't help but wonder how people spent so much of their time in a casino – trapped indoors, musty air, no connection to daylight or nature, and consumed by greed with the thrill of the chase in anticipation of a win.

Poker machine lights were blaring and loud noises echoed across the room, interspersed by screams of wild triumph when someone made a big win, or groans from losses too much to bear for others. I felt like I was in a tornado of artificial sound and light and life. I enjoyed one glass of bubbles to celebrate being in Monte Carlo, and then when the time came to head back to the cabin, I was the first on the bus.

* * *

The next morning, the birds were chirping and the sun was out saying hello. I had recovered from my heat stroke and did not have a hangover – I had kept my promise. I rolled over to find that I no longer felt like my skin was being stretched more than it wanted to go. My once red skin had now blossomed into golden brown.

Stretching and lifting my head up, I looked around to see who else was awake, when I heard soft crying. 'Kimberly, is that you?' I asked quietly.

'Yes,' she replied.

I got out of bed straight away, bumping my head on my way out. Looking up at her, I immediately noticed that her face was covered in red spots. 'Oh my God, are you alright?' I asked, bewildered by what I saw.

Kimberly was sitting up in bed; her fingers were going crazy scratching her arms and legs. 'I don't know what's happened,' she said, crying some more, 'but I'm covered in bites. I'm so itchy. I don't know what to do.'

'Come on, hope out of bed and let me take a look,' I said, reaching to help her out of bed.

She was covered from head to toe in tiny little bites, almost like her whole body was one big, itchy bite.

'Let's go and see Jo,' I said. 'She might have some stuff we can use to help.'

It was still early as we left the cabin; the sun was only just starting to poke its head above the horizon. I hadn't bothered to look at the time; however, Jo's cabin was open to emergencies at any time, and this was an emergency.

I knocked quietly at Jo's door, as Kimberly kept scratching.

'Come in,' Jo called.

Jo had a cabin to herself; she was already up and dressed, packed up and immaculately clean.

Kimberly walked in first – she was still scratching.

'Kimberly, what's happened to you?' Jo said with a look of disbelief.

'Something has bitten me in the night, I think. I can't stop scratching and I've started to get all shaky with it too,' she said, tears now flowing again.

'Do you have any allergies?' Jo asked.

'None that I know of,' Kimberly replied through sobs.

'Oh darling, I hate to say this, but I think you have been bitten by bed bugs, or for want of another word – lice.'

'Lice!' we both bellowed at the same time.

'Yep, sometimes with so many people swapping beds so often, the beds can get lice in them. It's pretty common in hostels, especially in this heat,' she said, taking a sip of water from her bottle. 'Don't worry, the bites will go down in a couple of days.'

'A couple of days!!!!' Kimberly almost screamed. 'I can't live with these for a couple of days. Besides the fact that I look horrid, I can't stand the itching,' Kimberly said as she almost ripped off her skin.

'Don't worry, we'll get you some antihistamines and some soothing itch cream; it will help. Go and have a cool shower, not warm as that will make it itchier. And whatever you have had in your bed, we will have to rewash. Put everything into a separate garbage bag and we'll sort it out at our next stop.' Jo rummaged through her first-aid kit and popped an antihistamine into Kimberly's hand. 'Take this, the itching will reduce soon.'

Taking the tablet and some soothing cream, we slowly made our way back to the cabin. It seemed to take forever, as poor Kimberly had to keep stopping and scratching every second.

'You do realise that I'm going to have to rewash my entire bag. I washed it all yesterday and folded it on the bed and repacked my bag. Shit,' Kimberly announced, as we walked up the stair to the cabin.

By now the room was awake, and with our new-found friendship, we all pitched in and gave Kimberly a hand with her clothes. We all then decided that perhaps it might be a good idea to wash *everything* again from the cabin – just in case. I ran back to Jo to get some more bags.

Chapter 15

A TRUE CONNECTION

The flat road we were on suddenly showcased snow-capped mountains in the distance – we had arrived at the base of the Italian Alps. Taller than anything I had ever seen before, towering over us with an immense force, the Alps made me feel incredibly small on this planet as I looked upon them.

Needing petrol, we pulled into a service station. This time we were all allowed out.

Around the corner of the service centre, there was a tiny pizza place, which was connected to the building.

The line for the pizza was at least forty people long. Could this be right? We were stranded, in the middle of nowhere, and there were cars parked in every possible space, with a line to get pizza as long as for a ride at Disneyland.

'Here's the deal,' Jo announced. 'You are only allowed one piece of pizza, and you must have the correct money. You cannot buy another item when you get to the counter. You need to place your order as soon as you approach the counter, otherwise you won't get served. I suggest everyone line up as you will never eat pizza like this again.'

Could this be true? The best pizza in the world is here, by the side of the road at a service station?

'Okay, let's do what the lady says,' I said to Kimberly.

We all jumped off the bus, the boys of course made a run for it like teenagers, and the rest of us lined up and waited, and waited. No one cared though, as the scenery was exceptional. We all just stood in the line gazing up at the mountains before us.

Finally, it was our turn, after about half an hour. Three giant-sized pizzas lay before me. I started to salivate purely at the smell. One was a very traditional margarita – tomato base with mozzarella cheese and basil; one had a few scattered mushrooms; the other had a few pieces of salami thrown on top. My decision was quick and easy – I chose the margarita.

Kimberly, Andrea and I made our way to a small grassy area with napkins in our hands. Taking the first mouthful, I was instantly transported to a new world in my love for pizza. Groans of satisfaction came from every person as we all devoured each delicious piece. Kimberly's misery started to fade with the scrumptiousness of the pizza. The size of my piece was as large as a small-sized pizza back home.

The base was thin, flat, with a semolina sprinkle underneath, giving it a change in the texture. The tomato base, made from sun-ripened tomatoes that had been smashed delicately, was just enough so that the flavour of the tomato shone through. The bocconcini was all melted and hot, crisp in areas, gooey in others, and cooked to perfection making long and stringy vines as it was pulled through the air with every bite. It was so delicately mild in flavour so as to not overpower the tomato.

I could feel the warmth of the sun through the tomato with each mouthful, and feel the love with which the pizza had been made. I knew in that instant that pizza would never be the same for me anywhere else in the world. Jo was right – that pizza was quite possibly the best in the world!

* * *

The heat continued throughout the morning, just as it had every other morning of our trip. I knew we were in for another pounding hot day. This part of the journey was a bit longer than most. Everyone had crammed on cheerfully after our treat of pizza in the morning, but with no air-conditioning in our new bus and still no toilet, everyone quickly became cranky.

I found a seat all on my own in the middle of the bus. This bus was slightly bigger than the other bus. I wasn't sure how that all worked, but in this bus, we had spare seats. This was a comfort and a curse to me.

Andrea was sitting with some of the guys towards the back of the bus, and Kimberly was miserable and sitting down the front asleep – she needed to rest and recover. I didn't want to bombard her with my desperate need to feel accepted by having someone to sit next to on the bus like some teenager unable to find peace within themselves while alone. Full tummies and the heat had made everyone go to sleep.

The overwhelming sense of lonesomeness started to suffocate me once again, turning my mind to self-doubt and personal sabotage.

Loneliness, for me, brought about a bleak outlook on life. *What is the point of living this life if there is no one to share it with?* My thoughts overtook my reality as I stared absently out the window.

Meeting new people was always a bit daunting, but so far, so good. I had managed to make a few new friends. We had already been through ups and downs together, and I had managed to start to feel some sense of connection, but still, everyone was always talking to someone else and often not to me. *Do I really belong?*

I was like a random nomad in search of something bigger and stronger. What was it really that I was searching for? Was it love? Maybe if I started to love myself, I wouldn't feel so isolated. Would my ability to love others unconditionally become greater? To do this, though, I had to stop being so hard on myself, be true to myself, and value myself and realise that it was okay just to be me.

But was it? Maybe I was too self-conscious, too untrusting to give anyone permission to see the real me. The wall around my heart was difficult to break. None of the people on the tour knew my past, where I came from, or who I really was. They only saw who I was then, and I had lowered my standards significantly since my formative years. I guessed that it was time to raise the bar again, and be the person that I could be proud of.

Perhaps it was not so hard in a new place to meet new people, where everything was already new, and when you could be whatever it is you wanted to be. But what did I want to be? I was still trying to figure that one out, but it certainly wasn't what I had been in recent times.

Solitude can often invite deep thought, reflection and transformative change, and now was the time to embrace the opportunity for that and find what I was looking for; however, all I was craving was companionship.

I used to love the quiet alone time back on the farm, sitting in my special place, soaking up the peace as it floated through me. But on the trip it was different. I no longer had the inner peace I once had, and although many others, who were no longer strangers, surrounded me, the feeling of disconnection and isolation within myself seemed to become even more apparent on this bus. The feeling of being lonely was more extensive than I could fathom.

My soul felt barren with the sinking feeling of isolation engulfing me. And the drinking, well that wasn't fixing anything; it was just putting a bandaid over the scared person that I was deep down. I was lost, lonely and confused. Would I ever find someone who I connected with? Who accepted me, just for me? Someone who understood me, all of me, even the parts of me that were lost?

Still unable to find the parts of my missing puzzle piece to feel whole again, I wondered if they would ever show up? And if I ever did make a true connection with another, would that be one of the missing puzzle pieces?

I had no idea.

Why did I have such a strong desire to feel connected to another? And now, with everyone asleep on the bus, it was only the gentle rhythm of their souls breathing and the familiar hum of the bus engine that kept me company.

I breathed deeply.

With my face in my hands, I rested my head on the windowpane; the heat from the day outside penetrated my forehead. I turned to look out the window at the scenery before me, trying to forget the thoughts in my head.

Never before had I seen scenery like this – the yellowing green rolling hills with the summer sun burning off the grass, little terracotta villas scattered around the hills surrounded by conifers? Evergreen and dark emerald in colour, they were tall and narrow like a pointy arrow heading up to the pale blue sky, lining dusty driveways and boundaries of land.

'My God, it is beautiful,' I said out loud to myself.

The terracotta was nothing like a terracotta pot back home, as somehow when the sunlight shone on it, it showed a different colour that resulted in a warmer, tangerine colour, making everything seem to fill with nourishing golden light.

I wish I could share this with someone. Mum would love this.

The thought of my family was another reminder of my loneliness.

Don't think of home. Tears filled my eyes. *Keep moving forward.* I experienced a small niggle of the unknown and that unsettled feeling in my gut rose.

Breathing in my tears, I wondered if there was anyone on this bus who I could share this with. *You're all missing this!* I yelled in my head once more. I wanted to yell at everyone and show them what they were missing.

I reached up, holding onto the back of the seat in front of me with both hands to support my weight. I looked around and saw a girl straight ahead. *Yes, someone else is awake! Someone I haven't really spoken to. Her name is Cassandra, I think,* The prospect of sharing this moment with someone stopped my tears and brought a smile.

I signalled for her to come up to me and that I had a spare seat.

'Okay,' she mouthed. Slowly, she wriggled out of her seat, so as not to wake up her fellow passenger. She then tiptoed up the bus towards me.

'Hi,' I whispered.

'Hi,' she whispered back, smiling. Her strawberry blonde hair glowed in the sunlight as it streamed in through the window. Her face was soft and kind, with big, bright blue eyes. She sat down gracefully on the chair next to me.

As she settled into the seat, a feeling washed over me like I had known her my whole life, even though I'd never spoken a word to her before. Sure, I'd seen her around, hanging out with her fellow travellers and having a great time, but we had never communicated.

Cassandra's smile was intoxicating; I couldn't help but smile too. Then we started talking, just the two of us, like little girls in kindergarten, whispering secrets to each other. We started sharing our lives, our heart-breaks, our losses and our joys. Laughter and tears fell out of us, like a waterfall spilling over a cliff face, while the bus motored through the valleys of Tuscany.

In the distance, conifers continued to shoot up out of the earth, like new seedlings coming up in the spring, among old villages rusty with age and lined with cobblestone paths, filled with families living their lives and carrying on as they did the day before. But to us, this day was new, this moment was new, as we formed a connection, one I had only dreamt of, and all while the Tuscan sun shone down on us like a light from heaven.

Every truth I knew about myself fell into her arms as she opened her heart to me and I to her. There was a spiritual connection running through our veins. Both of us felt it.

Some would say that our connection was destined, with our lives reunited from a previous life. Some might say it was simply by chance that a higher force had brought us together, or maybe it was God. Whoever it was or whatever it was, we had been pushed together onto this path that neither of us knew how to navigate.

But one thing we both did know was that we were each on a path of self-discovery, and now we were on that path together. She was the sister I had never had. She was my kindred spirit.

Chapter 16

FREEDOM

Giant deciduous trees fluttered in the heat of the summer breeze, snippets of sunlight shone down onto the road though their foliage which had created a natural made ceiling of the road – the heat had finally dropped, but only by a few degrees.

Cassandra and I walked up the hill towards the lookout, which was said to be spectacular. With determination and a new-found strength, I made it with ease as my heart had lifted and my self-sabotaging voice was slowly vanishing. It had been one foot in front of another on the journey so far, but as I looked up through a ceiling of leaves and the dappled sunlight shimmering on my face, I stopped and smiled. I could feel its warmth comforting my weary, aching soul as it slowly started to defrost. I was starting to feel easier within my own skin, maybe I could do this thing called life a bit easier. Maybe I was finding my own joy, underneath the canopy. A few more steps forward, I found my spring and caught up with the others.

As we reached our destination, the view in front of us spanned across what seemed like all of Tuscany, with Florence placed below our hill climb, its impressive dome tower Piazza del Duomo sitting erect in the background, and the Fiume Arno running peacefully through the city under famous bridges. Terracotta roofs lined the winding streets housing millions of pigeons. It all felt unfamiliar yet warm, gentle, kind and embracing. The robust nature of the Italians, their loudness and magnanimous nature in life, filled my soul just that little bit more.

The whole group bunched together to have our photo taken – I could see my new friends becoming a part of my new life.

'Say cheese!' Jo called out.

'CHEEEEESE!' everyone called, giggling like kids having their photo taken at school.

Another treasured memory had been made, yet this one felt different – change was coming within myself.

Wondering around our cabin site in Florence, I made my way to Cassandra's cabin. I hadn't been to her cabin before or anyone else's, only my own. I hadn't been invited. Cassandra and I had arranged to catch up before dinner; I was to meet her at her cabin.

Knocking tentatively on her door, I felt nervous. *Will she still want to be my friend? Maybe she was just bored on the bus? Maybe I told her too much? Maybe she doesn't really like me, and I just imagined everything?* I felt like the new girl at the new school. A tingle of fear was creeping in again; I tried to shoo it away.

Knock, knock.

'Come in,' I heard her call.

Nudging the door open, I saw her standing there with the same huge smile greeting me.

'I've got some vodka and soda,' she said, pulling out two paper cups.

'Great,' I said as relief washed over me and I realised that everything I feared seemed to only be in my head. 'Where are your friends?'

'Oh, they went off somewhere. Come sit down,' she said, pouring us both a drink, before we squished in beside each other on the step at the door of her cabin.

Instantly words started sprawling out of us – again – just as they had on the bus. It wasn't a once-off. The conversation flowed with both of us giggling in unison as we sat on the doorstep.

Our laughter started drawing attention from others within the camp-site. By the time it was dinner, a large group had formed around us, sitting around the doorway – the bottle of vodka now finished and another one started.

I was no longer wandering over tentatively to others. Now others were coming over to spend time with me – with us. The guard that was protecting my broken and shattered heart started to fall away a little. I felt stronger, more myself in some strange way. I felt settled. I didn't need to be someone else, something else, something that someone else thought I should be or anything other than just me.

I finally felt free.

***

The ancient presence of Rome was awe-inspiring. The Colosseum was crumbling underneath pounding tourists' feet. I felt privileged to be a witness to this ancient masterpiece of architecture, yet also an intruder. I could imagine the lions, elephants, tigers and other exotic animals roaring against the 50,000 spectators that the Colosseum housed once upon a time. Priests, emperors, politicians, men and women mired in poverty – from every walk of Roman life – once cheered alongside each other at someone's impending death.

Entertainers mingled among the tourists, dressed up in Roman costumes playing out battle scenes and providing some light-heartedness to this otherwise dooming space from ancient history.

Brick buildings were slowly decaying over time as thousands of years of natural and human torment eroded them. We had nothing like this in Australia, with European settlement dating back just over two hundred years and our Indigenous culture dating sixty thousand years, the majority of their existence ruined by English invasion. I wondered what was there before the rise of Rome?

It all felt so incredibly foreign to me, invoking another moment of inward reflection. *What is my purpose on this earth? Who am I?* My brain hurt with the scale of these questions about my life. I needed a diversion.

I took off on my own, leaving the group to explore more history than my brain could absorb. Wondering the streets aimlessly, I desperately tried to get some head space. Not a breeze moved one leaf in the city. It was stifling. I had no idea where I was going, only that I needed to breathe and keep moving.

Rome was filled with many marble statues surveying your every move. At first, you noticed their superior presence, but after a while, they start to blend in with the rest of the city and somehow seem to fit in with its modern-day mopeds and masses of people. Maybe this was the way Rome had always been, filled with masses of people and transportation of some kind. And the men, well that was a whole new ball game.

'Ooooh another gelato cart!' I said out loud to myself, excited by the possibility of cooling down with a tasty treat, and using it as a deviation while I tried to ignore the constant bombardment of name calling from the Roman men: 'Bella this . . .' 'Bella that . . .' It was starting to get under my skin.

A man stood at the gelato cart; he was tall, olive-skinned, dark hair, dark eyes, he looked Roman, like most of the other men walking the streets, not at all unattractive. Speaking to me only in Italian, I presumed he asked what I would like. I pointed to the pistachio, of course. I was making it my mission to find the best pistachio ice cream in all of Europe. Handing over the money, his every second word was 'Bella', and his body language indicated that he wanted more than my money – there seemed to be no language barrier when it came to physical attraction. I was not at all attracted to him. I did not want to be an object of desire to him or any man in Rome, or to any man in general. I was searching to find me – lust and desire were the last things I needed to find.

I looked at his dark liquid eyes, smiled my bright Australian smile, snatched my gelato – with more force than was necessary – and said, 'In your dreams, pal!' Then I turned abruptly and stormed off, head held high and filled with pride. I had done it. I had not fallen for his flattery. I didn't need his words or body language to tell me that I was more than sexual pleasure, that I was something in this world. I didn't want to jump into his arms and run off into the sunset, stealing myself away into the abyss of love. I wanted none of it. I just wanted my ice cream, and that was it.

I sat on the edge of a fountain around the corner from the gelato vendor, smiling like a kid in a candy store. I couldn't keep my pride to myself – all those years of being that downtrodden girl while I was with Patrick, I remembered that I didn't need a man to make me feel valued. Deep within my soul, I was finding *me*. I knew I hadn't actually lost who I was – I had just gone on holiday for a little while.

I wanted to run up to people and tell them. 'I AM MORE.'

And this time, unlike so many times before, I honestly believed it.

✳ ✳ ✳

The north of Italy wasn't nearly as hot as Rome. We were now in Venice. It came to us in a cool breeze off the water. We were staying in another cabin site, filled with the same orange timber cabins that had started to feel like home.

Andrea, Kimberly and I were sharing a cabin again. We had even developed a ritual at each site now – striding over to our cabin, bags on our backs, claiming whichever bed the first person found, with the last person getting the last bed available, which was often the bottom bunk. The bunk beds were tiny, with such a small space between the top bunk and the bottom, you had to kind of roll over and slide out without sitting up so that you didn't hit your head. Small, square, pine side tables sat nestled between the bunk beds, unable to hold much more than a couple of bottles of water and an alarm clock – both a necessities.

The sunset shone vibrant colours of orange, red and purple, illuminating the skyline above the enormous trees that lined the campsite.

With a new city to discover, we took a new mode of transport and hopped on board one of the many watercraft transportation options to get us into the city of Venice.

We had a free day for roaming and adventuring. Starting in Saint Mark's Square, Piazza San Marco, with too many pigeons to count, I instantly desired to go to another place, any place, with fewer pigeons. People were standing around, letting them sit on their shoulders, heads, arms, anywhere the pigeons could perch, and they were feeding them. I have always called them rats with wings; I felt repulsed. Now don't get me wrong, I am an animal lover by all accounts, any form of animal I appreciate, but letting pigeons sit on my head, no thank you.

Apparently, my preferences were different to the thousands that swarmed to the square on a daily basis. I made off in search of a non-pigeon section of the city and a bunch of others followed. I now had more friends. My smile beamed within me as we meandered our way around the narrow streets of Venice together. You could see the water lines on the buildings; the water had dropped or was at low tide, the smell was rancid, as stale water covered every nook and cranny wherever we went.

Our gondola sat waiting for us. When we climbed on board, it was strange to get sea legs after having bus legs for so long. I plonked down on the hard, red wooden seat resting my arm on the edge next to the golden dragon statute that decorated the side of the gondola.

Venetian men seemed to be a bit more respectful than the men in Rome. Our gondola driver smiled at us with kindness as we all settled ourselves in for the ride.

We twisted and turned through watery alleyways tucked between buildings two to three storeys high. Ageing from their wet landscape, with what was once a vibrant city of majestic yellows, oranges, whites and red, it was now shabby and depleted, worn with age and erosion. The paint was peeling in many places on the window frames, doorways and walls, faded from time in the blistering Italian sun and violent storms of the sea.

As we peacefully made our way through the labyrinth of Venice, our gondolier began to sing. What a voice! His voice boomed through the city's whispers as it echoed throughout the passageways.

At the end of our ride, I realised I could tick another thing off my bucket list – taking a ride in a gondola.

With some free time from our group, Andrea and I decided to go adventuring through the long, narrow streets; a fresh wind blew against us. We wandered around for what seemed like hours. As shop fronts closed, the city fell asleep for siesta time. We forgot that we were in Italy, and like many other countries in Europe, the afternoon was the time for a rest.

Nothing was open, but we were starving and also quite possibly lost.

My feet ached as we made our way around the city, trying to find some way back to the river transit. Exhausted, both of us needed a break. We sat in a gutter outside a restaurant, hot, hungry and thirsty. Looking up, I suddenly saw a shining light – a water fountain.

'Praise the Lord!' I exclaimed. I took the longest most rewarding drink of my life. After I had practically drowned my insides, I noticed that all the shutters were opening up again. It was time to get back into the day.

The doors to the restaurant near us opened, and a tall, dark and handsome waiter greeted us. *'Bongiorno belle ragazze,'* he proclaimed as he got on with his work.

'Parli Englese?' Andrea asked in her best Italian.

'*Si,*' the waiter replied, gracing us with his big Italian smile again.
Andrea blushed.

'Can you please tell us how to get back to the closest Vaporetto stop?'
Andrea asked.

Finding our way back, we fell into the seats on the Vaporetto, shopping bags at our feet. We longed for a cold beer as we looked out at the beautiful city that moved in time with the moon and the tides.

The bar back at the campsite, like many of the other bars throughout our travels, was filled with people dancing and singing, as they did most nights. Grabbing a couple of beers, a few of us left the party for somewhere a bit more peaceful. We found our way to an area where a bunch of people had pulled out the square side tables from their cabins and were now using them as stools.

Everyone was gathered around drinking and chatting, with one person doing the 'beer run' back to the bar every now and then, some of the guys decided to play a prank on the beer runner. First, they stacked the small side tables on top of each other for them to have to sit on, but then we all realised that they stacked with ease.

We stacked as many side tables up as we had available, and soon our tower of half a dozen side tables stood tall and robust. In our drunken state, we were sure that nothing could knock down our leaning tower of side tables, and decided that we needed more.

Soon we were knocking on doors and stealing everyone else's side tables until we could find no more.

Standing beside our great achievement, we were a proud team of side-table warriors, creating the 'Tower of Side Table Pisa' for the whole camp to admire.

The last guy from the other bus group then came running around the corner, with what we thought was the lucky last golden side table to add to the tower. Four of the guys lifted the tower up gently, well as gentle as drunken guys could be, but their balance wobbled.

A hush fell over the on-lookers as the next side table was placed underneath.

With a wobble from the top and a groan from the weight, one of the guys yelled, 'It's gonna blow!'

All four boys lowered it to the ground, with a creak and a thud; the tower moaned.

'RUN!' called out another guy.

Like ants emerging out of a disturbed nest, we fled the scene. Timber crashed, as every side table shattered into pieces. Shards of timber flew everywhere, as did we.

'Your cabin is closer than mine,' I yelled at Cassandra as we made a run for it. Quickly going inside and resting against the back of the door, breathing heavily, we looked at each other and laughed so hard till our stomachs hurt.

'I wonder if they'll notice all the missing side tables?' Cassandra asked once we had finally got ourselves into a state of calm.

'Surely they would be stupid not to notice,' I replied. 'I reckon if they find out who did it, they'll be asking for us to pay for the damages.'

'Hmm, I think you're right.'

'Do you think it's safe to go out now?' I asked, yawning, as all the adrenaline that had run through my body was now gone and I was over-whelmingly tired.

'Yep, just don't go anywhere near "the scene",' Cassandra replied giggling, with her bright blue eyes wide open, pretending to look scared.

I felt like a spy – I opened the door slowly and made my way out of her cabin and walked back to mine, checking every path and over my shoulder as I went, so that I wasn't being followed. But the site was dead quiet. There was not another living soul around.

We had bonded with this bus-tour group since our first stay in Paris, and now even more so over the building and ultimate destruction of our tower, but little did I know that they too would also be a part of another event that had even more devastating consequences.

The next morning as we all got onto the bus, I wasn't the most hungover. In fact, I hadn't been in some time. I had started to control myself since Barcelona.

And this time, unlike any other, Jo started the morning with a berating before the bus even took off.

'I have been a tour guide now for some years and I am highly disappointed with this group. The complete disregard for property is appalling. If we find out who has vandalised the site, we will be laying charges.'

It was clear that she was furious at what had happened and quite possibly been raked over the hot coals herself for our actions. We never thought for a moment that the whole tower would tumble and fall and destroy every last side table. The bus fell into silence as we took off listening to *You only get what you give* again, which seemed extremely appropriate.

Chapter 17

A FEW LITTLE LUXURIES

Finally a hotel!

Vienna appeared to be far more sophisticated than some of the other European cities we had visited so far. To fit in with such sophistication, we were not staying at a cabin site, but in a hotel.

Our keys were handed out – Kimberly and I would be sharing a room. Opening the door, we walked in 'oohing' and 'ahhing'. Comfy-looking beds with crisp, clean white sheets grabbed out attention first, plus we had our own bathroom, which meant we didn't have to share with twenty or more other tourists. There was only a small square window looking out onto a car park, but we didn't care. We had sheets! No sleeping bags tonight.

Immediately I jumped onto the bed, waving my arms up and down like I was making a snow angel, or a sand angel (if I was back home). The freshness of the sheets immediately made me think of how much I had been missing a real bed, not just a bunk bed with a sleeping bag on it, potentially filled with lice!

'I bags the first shower,' Kimberly called out to me from the bathroom.

'Go for it!' I called, still relishing in the smoothness of the sheets against my skin.

Half an hour later, I was sound asleep, still lying on top of my bed.

Kimberly flicked me with her towel. 'Wake up sleepyhead, time to get ready.'

I soothed myself in a long, hot shower with little water pressure, but that didn't matter, as there was no one else in the room while I had a shower. I didn't need to wear my thongs – though I did out of habit, and little soaps, shampoo and conditioner lined the bathtub that sat underneath the shower. I decided to put in the plug and have a bath at the same time. When was the last time I had a soak in a tub? *Scotland.* I pondered that thought for a moment as I sat down with my knees bent up – it was more like a bucket than a bath.

Closing my eyes and feeling the water wash over me, I felt so different to when I had first started on this adventure. I began to reflect back on when this had all begun, when Kimberly banged on the door. 'You've got only fifteen minutes.'

Where had the time gone? Jumping out of my bucket bath and flooding the bathroom, I quickly got dressed and even managed to use the hairdryer, just because it was there and I could.

I looked in the mirror. What had happened to me? My hair, full of regrowth, was falling all over my face, in places it wasn't meant to. My curls were bouncy, but they were also entirely out of control. I was beginning to look like I had been in the wilderness for some months, which I would generally have no problem with if I had been in the wilderness, but I wasn't in the wilderness, I was in Vienna – a place of sophistication and beauty. *Dear God, why didn't anyone tell me how bad my hair was? I am in desperate need of a haircut!*

I pinned my hair back in some mismatched style; it would have to do for now. I put on my signature eye make-up, with my pink dress from Barcelona, and then headed out to our Mozart concert.

The hall was as sophisticated as the rest of the city – white exterior with an interior of giant ostentatious chandeliers hanging from the ceiling.

Taking our places on the hard wooden seats with a worn, red velvet cushion, I held my breath when the orchestra came on stage. Dressed in period costume, it made the whole audience smile. I could feel the passion of the show through the light and shade of the music. I closed my eyes and let the music run through me.

It transported me to another place – a place where women were regaled in eighteenth-century dresses, wearing corsets, with white painted faces, fluttering their eyelashes and sitting elegantly underneath oak trees with swans gliding by in the distant pond and reeds rustled against the cool summer breeze. Men were wearing white wigs; they were massive on their heads. They stood tall with hands behind their back, pacing the pond, golden brocades lining their long jackets of blue and green, with white stockings underneath their red britches.

As we left the concert hall, I felt a sense of peace. Resting my heavy head on the stiff clean sheets of my hotel room, I drifted into a contented, peaceful slumber.

Breakfast was the same but somehow much better in a hotel restaurant rather than the 'mess hall' at some of the cabin sites. Jo informed everyone over breakfast of the whats and wheres for the day, if people were so inclined. We had another free day – options were endless with an abundance of museums, art galleries, palaces and historic buildings to consume.

Cassandra was busy checking over plans with her travelling companions to visit museums and see the sights. Smiling and winking at her as I left the restaurant, she knew I would be off wondering aimlessly – 'living like a local' – while she was busy being a tourist.

Grabbing my cup of tea and toast, I made my way back up to my room. Munching on my toast, with loud crunches of the super crusty bread, I left a trail of crumbs on the way back to my room. Andrea was already in the corridor when I arrived.

'What are your plans for the day?' she asked.

'I think I'll go shopping. I've had enough of museums,' I replied, grinning contently. I was looking forward to finding out about this city my own way.

'Doing your "living like a local" thing, hey?' she responded.

'That's the one,' I said.

'Cool, I'll join you.'

The two of us headed out of the hotel together, jumped on a tram and hoped that it would get us into the central shopping district.

Strolling down the Mariahilfer Strasse, we were surrounded by four-storey historical buildings with boutiques on each corner filling our every shopping desire. The mall was exquisite. A quick turn left, we found our way up a flight of stairs and in front of us was a hairdresser. We both went in, and an hour later, we had no more dodgy hair! It was the best haircut of my life. Not only did I look improved, I felt improved – funny how a haircut can do that for you.

Back on the bus, we were a passenger down – one of the guys had had horrible pains overnight and decided to go back to London. Such a shame that he couldn't finish the tour, but then again, maybe the planets weren't aligning for him. My faith in the powers of the universe had grown stronger with all of the incidents that kept occurring throughout my travels. I felt like someone, or something, was trying to tell me some-thing, the only problem was that I had no idea what it was trying to say to me – perhaps I wasn't listening hard enough?

With my new hairdo, jeans and t-shirt, I was ready for our dinner out that night in a secret location. To get there, we had to travel through a forest so dense and thick it felt like a story from a children's novel. Little huts reminiscent of the Hansel and Gretel fairytale were scattered among the ferns as we made our way to a building that had a Tudor design, like the others huts, only this house was slightly larger.

German accordion music greeted us as we opened the heavy wooden door. Our feast of Austrian food was laid out before us, down long, narrow tables to sit around.

The night was filled with music, singing, dancing and laughter as we embraced the accordion, the local beer, and each other, which created a special bond between us all. It was something that couldn't be replaced under normal life circumstances. We danced the night away, and continued our merriment as we boarded the bus and danced some more till our feet ached. Happiness from belonging had filled all our souls in the forests of Austria.

Soon though all those little luxuries were taken away from us as we left Vienna, as we were back on the bus again – but this time, Andrea and I had fabulous hair!

∗ ∗ ∗

A quick pit stop on the way to Munich in Salzburg proved a thrilling treat for those of us who loved the movie *The Sound of Music*. There was an opportunity to sit in the church where the lead character – Maria – was married in the movie. Sitting in the back of the church, Fiona and I, huge fans, decided to sit and pray, just like Maria would have. We were giggling like kids on Christmas morning with the excitement of being there. While sitting there, I prayed for the rest of my puzzle pieces to be found to finally feel 'whole'. I knew I was on my way to finding them all, as I could feel it in my bones, but a little help from God wouldn't go astray.

However, God didn't find me through my search within Munich, with its grubby buildings, grey skies, terracotta roofs and clock towers. Hundreds of people stood around the Glockenspiel, a giant cuckoo clock, watching it do its songs and dances. My grandmother loved her cuckoo clock; she would have loved it. I was on a mission to find her a tiny cuckoo clock to take home for her. If you enjoyed cuckoo clocks, Munich was the place to be. Or if you loved beer, Munich was also the place to be – German beer halls where in abundance.

∗ ∗ ∗

The beer hall was packed as we entered, and we soon held full beer steins to clink together in celebration of life. Mostly, the hall appeared to be filled with Aussie guys, all ridiculously drunk, some of whom were vomiting out the front of the building as we walked in, then standing back up to go in for more. *Yuck!* The place reeked of stale beer and sausages.

The stage was set for traditional German slap dancing, cowbell ringing and yodelling. I felt sorry for the performers, as none of their audience gave a damn about them or what they were doing. I couldn't wait to leave the place. It was the tasteless and tacky side of German tourism and brought out the worst in Aussie guys. Standing, watching everyone carry on like a bunch of baboons, I started to get irritable and desperately wanted to leave the soulless place.

Eager to get out of Germany, I was first on the bus the next morning – everyone else was hungover to all hell, but not me this time! I was finally starting to settle within myself and feel confident with who I was and what I believed.

Climbing through the Alps, I looked out the window of the bus; I felt like climbing the mountains and being out there among it all. Pine trees covered the sides of the mountains, luscious and green. I felt invigorated with every breath as I stared at the magnificence of their presence. *Songs* from the movie *The Sound of Music* came to my mind, playing over and over in my head while I pressed my forehead against the glass to get the most out of the view, and once again I felt like *Maria*.

Rattle . . . rattle . . . bang . . . hiss.

Oh no! The bus started smoking.

Alex drove the bus over to a truck stop area with a public toilet and picnic bench seats. We had broken down – again. And this time, Jo and Alex decided that there was no hope in fixing the problem quickly. We had to wait until another 'new' bus arrived.

Once again the rules of the bus applied.

Jo called out in her loudest voice – she no longer had her

microphone – 'Guys, we have broken down again. We have called for a replacement bus. Until that time, we are stuck here. NO ONE is to leave the bus under any circumstances!'

Groans echoed throughout the bus, yet again. At least we had the beautiful mountains to look at while we waited, and waited, and waited. Hours passed, and not another bus ventured past us. By now, my bladder was full and I, along with others, was desperate to use a toilet. As the toilet on this bus didn't work either, as well as the air-conditioning, we were all downing water like no tomorrow.

I looked out the window longingly at the public toilets. We all kept asking Jo if we could go to the bathroom, but she was like a stern head-mistress and refused every request.

But I couldn't wait any longer.

I approached Jo, crossing my legs and bending over in extreme pain, and growled, almost in tears, 'Jo, I have been hanging on now for what has been hours. If you don't let me off this bus to use the toilet or pee in the bushes, I'm going to pee in a bottle. I can't guarantee that I will not get it all over the bus floor. I am in agony. I physically can't hold on any longer!'

Jo had been standing in the door of the bus to stop anyone attempting to get off. She looked at me with defeat in her eyes. 'Okay. You can go,' she said and moved out of the doorway so that others and I could get past.

Running to the toilet and breathing a deep sigh of relief once I had been, I thanked the Lord. The queue for the loo was now the length of the entire busload of people. We were all in the same position.

When we headed back over to the bus, Jo was barricading the door again, but this time on the road. 'It's too hot! Bugger the rules, who knows how long we'll be here. You're not going to run off anywhere; there's nowhere to run to unless you want to get lost in the mountains. Everyone stay outside and cool off for a while.'

Excitable sighs were exhaled as everyone walked around, stretching legs and finding shade as we continued to wait.

'Why do our buses keep breaking down?' Cassandra asked me as we headed over to a shady spot by the side of the road.

'God only knows,' I replied. 'Why do bad things keep happening on this trip? Not just the bus, but the whole damn time, weird and bad things keep happening to so many of us.'

We sat in the shade pondering our situation, and I couldn't help but wonder if all the 'problems' were signs to say 'Stop, do not go any further'.

The niggling feeling had continued to sit in the pit of my stomach since I first got on the plane, all those months ago. *Is it my intuition speaking to me? That sixth sense?* I couldn't work out why I felt like this so often. I was fed up with trying to understand it, choosing to eat a chocolate bar instead.

Chapter 18

I BELONG

The bus jerked with a sudden stop as we arrived at Hopfgarten, Austria, a small village nestled in the Brixental Valley. Making our way towards the chalet with our backpacks back on, and hunched over, we showed signs of exhaustion after our extensive delay. There were some excellent options for rest and relaxation, or adrenaline and adventure during the two days we had in Hopfgarten. The thought of rest and relaxation was tempting, but adventure sounded much more like how I was feeling.

The afternoon was sunny, providing a perfect opportunity to discover the village and go up the gondola to the top of the mountain. Single-seated open-air chairs went up and down the mountainside, across farms with farmers herding their cattle, all with cowbells on. Their magical music drifted underneath us as we floated overhead. The earth was carpeted once again with brilliant green grass all kept low by the grazing cattle. Winter ski runs were visible in every direction; it was a top destination for winter sports.

Andrea and I called out to each other as we made our way up the mountain. The view was spectacular, almost like you could see the edge of the world. More cows meandered around the hillside; I wondered where they went in the height of winter, probably in barns, just for them.

With our lungs replenished with pure mountain air, the entire busload was ready for a night out on the town. Venturing into the village, we made our way along the cobblestone streets with hardly any cars in sight. A few bicycles leant up against the shops and home fronts. The village was tiny, filled with traditional Austrian architecture. The houses were mostly two-storeys high, all with little square windows and shutters to help block out the cold in winter. Some had balconies, some had A-framed roofs, and all had orange-tiled roofs and no fences. The village felt friendly and safe – the villagers smiled at us as we made our way along the road.

Opening the door to a restaurant, we expected to see schnapps and beer. Instead the music was blaring *Great Southern Land* by Australian Crawl. Australian and New Zealand flags were hung high over the ceiling, and there was a boxing kangaroo banner on the wall and Fosters on tap.

'Dear God, we've walked into an Aussie bar!' I proclaimed to Cassandra as we entered.

The boys started cheering and headed straight to the bar, bursting into song. I looked around in sheer wonderment as to why a village in Austria would have an Australian bar.

Soon it all started to make sense as another tour group walked in, mostly Aussies and Kiwis. More cheers where heard as they made their entrance, and the same thing happened at least another two times during the evening. The beer was flowing with many of the boys performing exactly like the German beer halls – vomiting outside and coming back into the bar for more. I didn't understand how anyone could do that – they must have felt awful the next day.

Australian music continued to play as a thumping noise started in a dark corner of the bar. Everyone turned to look around to see foam spraying all over the dance floor. A foam party!

I had heard of these events but had never been to one before. Taking my shoes off I headed straight in, along with everyone else. Foam flew through the air, and I felt like a kid in a bubble bath. People were making beards with it, and some made hats with it, while others put it in places that made me hope that I'd never touch that particular foam again. People were slipping and sliding all over the place.

Then a girl who was not from our group hit her head sliding across the floor, cutting her head open and filling the foam with blood. One of her friends with an American accent called out, 'Call 911.'

There was a mass evacuation of the foam pit as everyone ran away from the injury and the now contaminated foam. Paramedics arrived and the girl was taken away, her friends following behind.

If I had hit my head, would any of my friends come with me to the hospital? I wondered. *Yes, they probably would – they saved me in the toilets in Spain.*

Getting a drink, Cassandra approached me. 'I'll have one too! Let's get this party started again,' she said smiling at me.

I finally realised that I did have friends who had my back, and I had theirs! I couldn't hide the smile from my face. I had made true connections and I felt blessed.

* * *

The next morning, adventure was upon us in the form of mountain bike riding. I had only been walking and dancing for exercise up until then. I was nervous about my level of fitness, and how I would manage to ride a bike up the side of a mountain, not to mention with a first-class hangover. The night before had gone well into the morning; I wasn't sure what time we had got in.

'God, I'd kill for a Coke,' I said out loud as I walked down into the mess hall for breakfast.

'Sore head?' said one of the guys who worked in the chalet.

'You could say that,' I said, rubbing my head.

'Vending machines over there,' he said, pointing to a Coke machine in the foyer of the chalet.

'You are a lifesaver.' I smiled, and then making my way ever so slowly to the vending machine, I reached into my pockets to find some coins.

'Oh no, I left my purse in my room,' I moaned. 'I can't make it up the stairs again.' I looked longingly at the stairs and back at the vending machine. 'Why is life being so unkind to me?' I said out loud, feeling nothing but sorry for my self-inflicted pain.

The guy walked over to me; he had long, straight, auburn hair tied up in a ponytail, and a long face that was covered with a red beard. 'Here you go,' he said, putting a couple of coins into the vending machine and choosing the option for a Coke.

The soft drink can hit the bottom, and groaning again, I went to pick it up and thought I might faint.

'You're in a bad way,' he said. 'Here you go.' He lent down and grabbed the Coke and handed it to me.

I managed a small smile with a tiny 'thank you', just audible enough to be heard.

Taking a sip, I could feel the icy cold liquid entering into my very unhappy tummy. 'I'll pay you back when I can manage to get back up the stairs,' I said pitifully. Then I started laughing at my pathetic excuse for not being able to climb the stairs. I wasn't in a wheelchair; I was hungover, it would pass.

I was determined to make the most of the day, no matter how hungover I was, as was Kimberly. We both felt nervous about the ride. Together we concocted a plan to stay together, even if one of us found it difficult. Everyone was assembling out the front of the building, finding their mountain bikes and getting all of their safety gear on.

The guy who had bought me the Coke was still at the front counter. 'See you later,' he said, chuckling to himself.

Nodding my head, I made my way outside, linking arms with Kimberly.

Helmets on, feet locked into place, we took off along a gravel path. As per usual, the boys carried on like teenagers, racing each other and making bets as who would reach the top of the mountain first.

How long had it been since I had been on a bike? Not since I'd lived with Patrick, when I had fallen off my bike riding up a hill and taken all the skin off my shin. A lady with small children had come out of her house and walked me back home as I was so shaken up. Patrick wasn't particularly sympathetic. I hadn't been on a bike since, more because it reminded me of him than due to a dislike of bikes. And now it felt like a distant memory – my bike, my crash and Patrick.

I smiled at myself, proud of how far I had come.

Cassandra stayed behind after her injury in Venice. She had torn a ligament in her knee from playing touch footy. No one, not even she knew how bad it was until we got to Germany, when she secretly took herself off to hospital and came back on crutches. Her adrenaline days were over for now.

Andrea had already sped ahead, calling out to us as she peddled with pace up the mountainside. Kimberly and I made our way up the mountain slowly and steadily. At first we kept up with the others, but as time wore on, our bodies and our hearts just weren't in it. It was hard work!

Stopping at what seemed like every kilometre, we kept encouraging each other to make it all the way, often getting off and walking our bikes just that little bit further, until finally, we reached the top. We were chuffed with ourselves – we had done it! Kimberly and I gave each other high fives as we hopped off our bikes, both of us giggling as our legs started to wobble slightly. The whole group had already made it, but by the looks of things, it wasn't so easy for them either.

Large umbrellas sat on top of picnic tables blocking out the sun and giving us a reprieve from our adventures. Lunch and a cold beer were ordered, as the ride seemed to have fixed my hangover. *Maybe I should take up mountain biking when I get home,* I thought to myself, but that idea quickly faded as I soon had to move and my legs had turned to jelly.

'Wait till you see how we get down,' Jo announced to us as she walked by. She must have seen the look on my face.

Jo was right; the descent down was nothing short of thrilling. I had never been so fast on a bicycle. We flew down the mountain like the Tour de France professionals, though I have to admit I was a bit scared at specific points, even though the adrenaline was pumping. Taking some of the turns, I thanked God for my motor-biking skills from back on the farm.

The bar in the chalet was far more impressive than in town. It felt more authentic with pairs of skis lining the timber walls, schnapps lining the bar shelves and current music pumping through the sound system.

The entire tour group made its way into the small space with shots poured and rounds bought. Kimberly and I decided to celebrate our dare-devil feat and do a round of shots. Though it wasn't any shot, it was schnapps, and at happy hour it was served in sets of six.

Shot after shot, Kimberly and I downed our drinks, to the point where the alcohol burned down our throat as it entered our system.

Everyone in the bar was singing and dancing. Our group had finally clicked. We all knew each other really well by now – where we were from, what foods we liked and didn't like, what types of adventures we wanted in life. We had all bonded throughout our experiences; we had all accepted each other, just the way we were, warts and all. We had shared in our plans for the future – what we would do when this trip was over, what we wanted for our life – but for now, we planned to enjoy every single minute, so that was precisely what we did.

The staff behind the bar were also on missions to enjoy themselves, including the guy from the front desk.

'He keeps looking at you – Mr Front desk!' Andrea commented.

Looking over, I saw who she meant – the guy who bought me the Coke. 'So what?' I said.

Andrea nudged me, winking.

No, I am no longer up for that. I am finding my way, without the need to be wanted by a man. I could feel that all too easy sense of attraction making its way into my body. It was his eyes; they appeared to be gentle, full of soul and laughter. *This is something I need to look for in a man when I am ready to meet a man who I can have a real life with, a real connection, an acceptance and a true love. But not now. Now I must find the rest of me, all of me, with no one else to find it for me. It must only be me who completes this journey.*

Chapter 19

MY LIFE AS BIG AS A MOUNTAIN

The river where our whitewater rafting adventures were about to commence was calm as we drove along the winding road. It ran along the bottom of a stark Austrian cliff face. Pine forests lined the edge of the cliff like miniature trees out of my Lego set from when I was a child; they were so high up, it was hard to distinguish their individual shapes, they just looked like tiny, pointy green things. Pulling into the gravel road, we saw wooden yellow huts covered in hooks upon which wet suits, life jackets and helmets hung neatly in rows ready for us.

Excitement started to build within the troops on the bus. Everyone's hunger for adrenaline was building.

We could hear the movement of the water peacefully flowing down the river, fast but not fast enough to pick up some rapids. We marched in line once we were all geared up and full of instructions. We stepped inside the red, rubber boat and launched into the river. The water was icy blue, with tiny bubbles of white foam collecting between the nearby rocks. The river was serene, about ten metres wide. I scooped my hand over the edge of the boat; the water was freezing, even though it was the middle of summer. The ice had melted to create this river. My fingers felt numb instantly. *God, I hoped I don't fall out. I'll freeze!*

Our guide pushed us off, steering us into the middle of the river. Everyone called out to each other in elation; we were all within a short distance of each other. Some of the crazy boys stood up in their rafts – *show-offs.*

I hung onto the yellow rope that lined the inside edge of the red, rubber boat, ready to take a twist or turn, but we just floated along peacefully. I started to relax and enjoy the scenery; there was little else to do. The river was nothing like the rivers at home; the water was not brown and murky with logs and branches bending to find relief from the hot summer sun. No dry patches from drought times revealing sandy bottoms and old parts of trees from floods long ago. This river looked like it had never had the desperation of drought in all of its history. Floods maybe, but no blistering forty-degree days soaking up every last drop of water from a mighty river that once flowed.

Our guide redirected us of a section that often had rapids on calmer days, though we continued to float peacefully over a bubbling section of the river. Our desires for adventure increased when the reality of not one single rapid to go through came into view as we could now see the yellow huts of the headquarters. We had come to the end of our journey. Disappointment filled all of our hearts as we disembarked.

'Never mind, there's always canyoning tomorrow in Switzerland,' I said.

Nods of agreement echoed across the river.

'I want a refund!' one of the girls called out. 'That was too easy? Where are the rapids?'

More nods followed, as we all looked in her direction.

There was nothing the company could do; it was Mother Nature showing a peaceful side of her. As much as I had enjoyed our float, I too was a little disappointed that there had not been more rapids. I kept my hopes up for the canyoning tomorrow.

✳ ✳ ✳

During a brief stop at Liechtenstein, the smallest country in Europe, we stretched our legs as we wondered the streets before heading into Switzerland, our next stop.

Stopping in Lucerne, Switzerland, we were greeted by a giant lion's head that was carved into the side of the mountain, which was surrounded by watch shops and chocolate shops. Giant Toblerones over a metre long were the purchase of choice, with the majority of the girls buying either one to take home or one to eat straight away. I chose to buy one to eat immediately, plus much smaller Toblerones to take home, as they were all in different flavours that you couldn't get back in Australia. I knew my brother would love them!

Kimberly, Andrea, Cassandra and I concocted a plan to stay in the same room together when we got to the chalet in Switzerland and share our chocolate! A girls' night in – pyjama party with cups of tea and giant chocolates – what more could a girl ask for? I didn't need the alcohol; I didn't need the men. What I had been searching for, and what I had been missing was friendship, companionship, and acceptance.

To get to our next stop, we had to make our way around Lake Brienzersee. Piercing blue sky covered the landscape as impressive mountains climbed up to the heavens – its rock faces were covered in snow at the top. It took my breath away.

Heading down the driveway into our accommodation, we were surrounded by the Swiss Alps on either side of the village that lay below. Cascading waterfalls tumbled over the cliffs of the Alps, falling harmoniously in time with nature. The town seemed so tiny sitting below the immense cliff faces that scaled the edges of the Alps.

I felt microscopic on the earth while looking out of my bedroom window, staring up at the Alps; they were so big, and I was so small. The air was pure and clean and crisp, as I breathed in the life of the mountains. I had fallen in love.

Grabbing the cold-climate clothes that I had been lugging around the whole of Europe with absolutely no use for until then, I raced down the stairs. I didn't want to be late for the opportunity to be a part of anything. My next adventure was a trip up to Jungfraujoch. I headed out with a woollen jumper and leather jacket in hand. It was hard to believe that in a short time I would need these and would possibly still be cold . . .

We climbed on board the train that was to deliver us to our destination. It chugged along, rattling and clanging, noisily, which added to the atmosphere. With the windows down, I stuck my head out the window, taking in long deep breaths. I felt alive!

The green of the mountainside was so vivid you needed sunglasses. Barns with orange roofs hid in the side of the mountain, while old men with long, white beards walked their cattle through the pastures with canes in their hands.

A glacier lay between mountain peaks, like a slice of heaven just sitting there, waiting. The iridescent green of the mountainside, with its Lego pine trees scattered in the distance, started to fade into rock faces and white chunks of cold. Snow! I had never seen snow in real life. Sleet, hail, rain, thunderstorms, floods, droughts, fifty-degree-days, deserts, surf beaches and reefs had all been part of my life. But never snow. And this snow was some of the oldest snow on the planet.

We were 3454 metres above sea level. I looked out at what the world must have looked like in the ice age. The air hurt my lungs with its intense cold. Fluffy clouds of snow nestled into the side of the mountains, the ice sea making its way between them for thousands of years, untouched.

I needed to experience it, feel it for myself, just a little bit, to know I was there, in that place of wonder. It was a place so untouched; I could feel its essence. I made my way down the metal staircase, ropes and cables making it steadfast – it felt like it could withstand the most violent of blizzards – moving in time with the hordes of tourists, all feeling the same as me. Privileged.

And then I touched it, for the first time, snow. Holding it in my hands, feeling its cold melting between my fingers was a thrill. It felt like it had washed away all the torment of the years gone by from my life with Patrick, when I had lost so much of myself, and now I was there, almost reaching the clouds, close to God. I felt renewed; my life was all starting to make sense.

My life was as big as this mountain. It had history but would continue on, no matter what happened. If this ice could withstand Mother Nature's force, so could I. The ice was my puzzle piece. The piece I had been searching for.

Standing alone, out on the ice, looking out to the glacier, I tilted my head back and screamed at the top of my lungs.

'I AM FREE.'

'I AM ME!'

I was liberated and it felt fantastic!

* * *

That night, excitement filled my soul knowing that I was moving forward on my own, but now also with a tribe, a sisterhood who had nothing but acceptance of me. But above all, I finally had acceptance of myself.

I needed to share with my family my news – I was finally the 'me' I had been searching for.

Hearing Dad's voice, my heart skipped a beat.

'Hi Dad!'

'Possum!' he replied excitedly. I could hear his smile. 'Where are you?' I felt his love and warmth through the telephone line.

'Dad, I'm in Switzerland!' I was sure he could hear my smile too.

I told him about my adventures, the mountains, the disappointing whitewater rafting and all the fun I was having with my new friends. I spoke dreamily of what was to come tomorrow, canyoning, and my plans for moving to London, and who knew what else was in store for me. Whatever it was, I was ready.

Most importantly, I told him how I was making the most of every moment, living in the present and felt whole and complete.

'Dad, I'm having the best time. I feel alive.'

'That's wonderful, possum; it's what you went there for after all.'

'Dad, you would love it here. One day, you and I, we'll have to come here together. I love you, Dad.'

'I love you too, possum.'

The line fell silent – Australia was gone for now. Home still remained a place filled with encouragement and love as it had always been, and as it had always been within myself. And now I knew it. I'd found my missing puzzle pieces. I felt whole and comfortable in my own skin. I was ready for my next steps. And they were the steps back to my room.

All the girls were waiting for me – Andrea, Kimberly, Fiona, Sasha and Cassandra. Already in their pyjamas, they were looking longingly at our enormous pool of chocolate. They had waited for me. Smiling, I grabbed my PJs and my giant one-metre Toblerone, adding it to the pile.

Giggles come out of our room for hours on end as we made our way through our own private mountain of chocolate. The sisterhood solidified in those hours; we all knew that we had created a bond so strong that nothing could break it. We had made friends for life, and all of us relished in this discovery of the love that we all felt for each other.

I'd found my tribe.

Feeling like schoolgirls being incredibly naughty, we ate chocolate after chocolate, finally falling asleep with sick tummies full of yummy Swiss goodness and enormous hearts.

The sun shone through our curtains the next morning.

Kimberly was standing in the middle of the window, pulling them open with force. 'Look at that everybody. Look at our morning!'

Stretches and yawns commenced, as we let the sunlight shine in on our souls.

'It's going to be a great day today!' I said, jumping out of bed.

We all made our way down to breakfast, still giggling, linking arms and singing through the hallways. Bright and happy, we were filled to the brim with happiness. Lots of us were heading in different directions for the day – some were having a day of free time, relaxing or visiting the local village – including Kimberly, Andrea and Cassandra. The others were going canyoning, including me, and there wasn't much time before the bus left. We needed to be swift in whatever activity we chose.

I had decided that I needed to buy Swiss army knives while in Switzerland, one for dad, Matthew and myself! The rule was, when you were out on the farm, fixing fences or doing farm work, you always had your Swiss army knife with you.

I was so excited to see that they were different to the ones back home. All you could get in Australia were red ones, but there were so many colour options in Switzerland. I knew they would love this gift.

Looking up at the clock, I only had fifteen minutes to get back to the coach. Grabbing my gifts, I made a run for it like my life depended on it.

'You only just made it – again,' Cassandra said, winking at me as she stood by the door watching everyone pile onto the bus.

'Can you pop these in my bag, please?' I asked, throwing her my bag of goodies before racing off in the direction of the bus.

'Sure thing,' she called out to me as I took off. 'Have fun. See you when you get back!' Cassandra waved frantically, but with a look of sadness as the bus took off. She couldn't partake in our adventures – again – but maybe she was never meant to.

Chapter 20

CHOOSING THE LIGHT

It was becoming a bad habit of mine, nearly missing the bus. After another close call, I made it to Adventure World, the company taking us on our canyoning tour. What seemed like hundreds of wetsuits hung in the equipment room, alongside helmets, life vests and wetsuit boots, which were all laid out for us to find our size and put on. With my wetsuit on, I looked in the mirror, noticing how frizzy my hair had become. *Is it going to rain?*

We stood outside Adventure World headquarters while the guides gave us a brief introduction on canyoning. One of the girls revealed that she thought we were going 'canoeing', but this was nothing like canoeing. *If it is anything like yesterday's rapids, or the creek back home, we will be fine.*

I looked up to the sky and I could see a storm brewing in the very far off distance – it seemed such a long way away. I wondered, though, if the rain was near where we were headed.

Looking out at our large group, I hoped that everyone had actually listened carefully to all the safety details for what we were about to embark upon. There seemed to be tension in the air, an apprehension of what we were about to undertake – it seemed as if none of us really knew what canyoning was. We all walked off in our smaller groups, which had been formed in no apparent manner. I wasn't concerned who was in my group; I was doing this for me.

It seemed a long way to the gorge from Adventures World's headquarters. We travelled along, winding roads that were surrounded by tall trees pointing straight up like gigantic pins heading to the sky. There were thousands of them, some in rows and others scattered randomly from the spray of seeds caught in autumn winds. These trees were magnificent up close.

I looked out the window of the minibus; the forest appeared darker the further ahead I looked. So dark that it seemed to be lifeless inside, like in the depths of the ocean, when it is so black that only specific sea life can live there. These forests had that same sense of mystery as the depths of the ocean. I imagined that there would be mystical creatures within the forest, submerged by green leaves.

I opened the window to let in some of the woodland air. It was fresh and smelt of earth, clay and pine, with a hint of rain. I filled my lungs and felt invigorated by the oxygen that was surging through my body. I felt healthier, stronger and taller, like the trees around me.

'Close the window, it's cold,' one of my fellow passengers called out to me.

'Can't you smell the forest? It smells amazing. Fill your lungs with this pure, clean air,' I replied.

'Don't care; it's cold!'

I closed the window with a thud and stared out the window. *How can they not be filling themselves with this beauty?*

In the distance, I saw the same clouds I'd seen earlier, only now they were dark and threatening. The clouds brought me back to thoughts of home. I always knew when we would get rain, besides the telltale signs from my hair. The weather patterns were always something a farmer learnt about at an intimate level – which direction the weather came from, what way the wind was blowing, the type of clouds that would deliver the promise of a downpour to fill up the dams. But here, everything was different, upside down, and I had no idea about these clouds or if they were anything like the ones back home.

A squeal of joy from the back of the bus jumped me back into reality. The energy in the bus was one of anticipation and excitement, with adrenaline starting to flow through our veins. Our trip was coming to an end; we were all excited about what adventures lay ahead for us and what would happen for the remainder of the trip.

I was planning to take up my new London friend's offer and move in with them for a while. Hopefully, she would remember me. I'd get a job in a bar somewhere in London, or maybe with my friend from the resort, save up some money and keep travelling. Skydiving somewhere in England was on my radar. All the sights and smells of such an unfamiliar place had affected me deeply – I had the travel bug, and it wasn't going to end in a couple of days when the tour was over.

'The bars in Brussels were fabulous and worth a visit. Awesome beer,' one of the guys said.

Typical, always thinking of beer, and here we are among some the world's most prestigious mountains, and all you can think if is beer. Pfft! I rolled my eyes as I stared back out the window.

'If ever I died today . . .' I heard one of the girls saying.

I tuned off. *Who would talk about dying? No one's going to die.*

I kept staring at the forest. But the comment unnerved me. I felt the tiniest sense of butterflies in my tummy again. I sensed a strange form of fear sneak into my intuition, but I was so good at ignoring it; I looked out to the clouds and turned it off once more.

I looked up at the sky again. *Will we get that rain or will it blow over the mountain? If we do get the rain, how will that affect where we're going and what we're doing? It looks a long way away.* I trusted that our guides knew the area well enough to know when things were safe or not.

Still, the butterflies in my tummy grew and grew.

I felt uncomfortable with my wetsuit sticking to my body and holding my helmet on my lap while being crammed into the little minibus. I was starting to get carsick as the road twisted and turned, like my stomach.

Keep looking at the sky. But the sky had vanished behind the mass of dark, emerald green forest canopy; the lights to the minibus went on as it became instantly dark. All the voices from the bus vanished as I slowly started to drift off to sleep in a desperate attempt not get carsick. *Maybe that's why my tummy is feeling upset? I'm just carsick – it's not my intuition.*

I was in denial – again.

We finally pulled over to a clearing and we all scrambled out of the bus like ants from an ant hill being trampled on. My feet hit the ground; it was a sealed road, not a dirt road like forest roads back home. *They must use this area a lot for it to be a sealed road.* I looked around; it was getting darker by the minute. No one else seemed to have noticed the weather or the light changing; they were all too busy chatting among themselves.

We seemed to be quite a way up the mountain, maybe halfway up. I wasn't sure how long I had slept, or how long it had taken us to get to our destination. The guides had moved away from our group and appeared to be having a very serious discussion.

I started to put my life vest on while watching everyone doing the same. One of the other girls was also taking note of the weather and looking around with a look of concern. *Does she have butterflies like I do?*

'Okay guys,' said our guide, 'here's the deal, we're not sure whether or not we should go in today, due to the rain, but it should be okay. There are exits all along the canyon so we can get out at any stage if we think it looks like we can't proceed for whatever reason.' He looked around waiting for a response.

No one said anything.

'Follow our lead, and let's get going. We might have to move quicker than usual so that we miss the rain. Follow me in single file.'

Falling into single file, we walked behind our guide, everyone talking and getting louder as we left the road and started to head down into the canyon via a highly visible dirt path. Giggles and shouts of excitement could be heard echoing through the forest from enthusiastic adventurers. I was watching every step I took, as my rock shoes were not that sturdy. I stayed at the back of the line. Everyone had their friend that they had travelled with by their side. I was alone, and this time I was okay with it, in fact I didn't even care.

'First jump of the day,' announced the guide. 'It's not really a jump, but more of a slide. An all-natural slippery dip, so do as I do, sit on your butt, hold onto the rock here and here.' He sat down on the edge of some rocks, where crystal-clear water flowed down into the canyon and out of sight. Looking over his shoulder, he bellowed, 'Give yourself some leverage, and when you let go of the rocks, lie down with your arms across your body as you slide down. You will then end up in a waterhole. Swim over to the edge when you land. We will tell the next person when to go.' And with that, he let go of the rocks on either side of his body and was out of sight in a flash. We could hear him calling out, 'Yahoo!' as he slid down.

A giant splash vibrated against the boulders, then his voice echoed from deep inside the canyon, 'Next! Off you go.'

The first person jumped up and took off screaming out 'yahoo' as they went down the natural water slide. It looked like fun, just like when we went swimming in the creek at home. Though, it was significantly steeper than back home. There were sandstone boulders and water so clear and pure you could drink it. Moss was growing over the ground by the rocks creating a carpet of velvet green.

I couldn't see where the edge of the mountain was – we were so deep in the forest, about halfway up the mountain. The sky was becoming darker as the clouds were closing in on us; I could hear thunder in the distance. The sound of the storm seemed to be at least four or five kilometres away from what I could work out. Only I just didn't realise that the storm was actually on top of the mountain we were on. And soon the storm would come for us.

My turn came; I put my foot into the water. I could feel the force of the current, it was strong, but that was nothing to worry about, it just meant I could go down the slide faster. I put my hand in the water, cupping it and lifting the water up into the air to see its clarity – it trickled between my fingers and glistened like a diamond, catching all the colours of the rainbow in what little light there was left. I sat down slowly, careful not to slip on the wet rock and grabbed hold of the boulders on either side of me. Giving myself a thrust, and with a push from the guide behind me, down I went, arms over my chest, slipping and sliding like on a toboggan, but without the device. It was just me, the water and the rocks.

With a whoosh and a splash, I landed in the waterhole. I couldn't wipe the smile off my face. 'That was awesome!' I called out as I swam, gliding over to the water's edge like a freshwater mermaid. I loved to swim, and this was no exception. The pool was icy cold and dark at the landing spot from how deep it was, but it was clear, so, so clear. I wasn't sure I had seen such a picturesque and pure natural space, beaming with the life of ferns and trees licking at the water's edge. It was a scene from a postcard.

I pulled myself out of the water, and I could see that all the others were beaming just as much as I was.

'Next jump – this way,' I heard the first guide say as the last guide made his way down nature's slippery dip, landing with a bigger splash than any of the others.

'Show-off,' a girl called out from the group.

Everyone laughed.

I turned around to take in one last look at this mountainous Garden of Eden. I saw circle patterns being made in the now still water. *Is that fish or rain? Fish this high up on the side of the mountain, is that even possible?* I held my hand out to see if I could feel anything. I couldn't on my body – I was covered from head to toe in wetsuit material. Yes, it was rain, but it was only spitting. I looked up at the sky. I could feel a gentle sprinkle of rain on my face. I closed my eyes feeling another aspect of the earth in this special place.

The dirt path ended abruptly on top of a boulder where our next jump would take place. Looking down at the canyon, I could see a gentle stream running quietly between rock faces, where more luscious ferns stuck out of the earth, reaching up into the filtered light, and still we were surrounded by tall, intimidating pine trees that must have been hundreds of years old.

'This jump is not really a jump. We are abseiling down the side of this boulder and into the next waterhole,' the guide explained.

'Brilliant, I love abseiling!' I said out loud.

A girl from the group looked positively terrified.

'Don't worry,' I said, 'it will be safe and heaps of fun.'

'It's not the safety I'm worried about,' she said. 'I'm scared of heights.'

'That's okay,' I said with a smile, 'you don't need to look down, just look straight ahead at the rock face. You won't even know you are up high.'

One by one, we connected ourselves to ropes and harnesses and made our way down the rock face, some jumping off the side of the boulder with joy, others with trepidation, and some needing gentle coaxing.

I stood on the edge, ready to make the jump. Once I had the go-ahead from the guides, I jumped freely, hearing the whir from the ropes against the carabiners and feeling the adrenaline surge through my system. I landed both feet against the hard rock, jumping again and again until I hit the water. I was down within thirty seconds, or at least it felt like thirty seconds; it wasn't such a big jump after all, but super fun.

I beamed looking back up at the boulder, and then I unlocked myself from my harness, ready for the next person to sail down. I thought about how I'd always loved abseiling as a kid and was so excited to be doing it again. I then started to wonder why I'd never done more outdoor stuff. *Well, now is the time. I'm going to start getting involved in more adventurous activities when I get home.*

I watched on as all the others landed, and then we moved onto our next stage with a little more urgency from our guides.

We waded through the water in single file; the boulders had started to close in on us as we weaved our way through the canyon. The air had cooled, and I'd notice that the water had gone from crystal clear, to brown and murky. *Is it just because it's from a different part of the canyon?* I didn't really think so. Too many years of living in the country and understanding floodwaters, teaching kids survival water skills at school, I knew that this was not good. I started to get concerned, for not only was the water changing colour rapidly, but it was also rising, going from ankle depth to above my knees from the time we entered into the crevice in the canyon.

'Why is the water rising?' the girl in front of me asked, obviously as concerned as I was.

'I don't know,' I said, 'but I'm worried.'

'Me too,' she replied.

We both looked around with fear in our eyes.

The guides were really trying to get us to hurry now.

'Okay!' one of the guides yelled, 'who wants to go first?'

Instantly I yelled out, 'I do.' Something inside me knew I had to get out of there and fast. I never put my hand up to go first for anything, but this time, it was my turn to take the first leap. My intuition took over, and instinctively I listened to it. I moved without even realising what I was doing.

I scrambled desperately past all the participants of my group and climbed up a rope that was locked into place by a giant nail in the rock.

The guide standing by the nail in the boulder started yelling instructions to me of how this next jump would work. I could hear waves crashing, the sound vibrating between the boulders further up in the canyon. It grew louder by the second, suddenly sounding like the ocean, not a creek. I could hardly hear the guide.

'You're going to free jump into the waterhole, right where the guide is below. It's a very narrow landing – miss the spot, and you'll break your legs. You've got a metre squared area to land in,' he yelled.

Right, it's now or never.

Taking a large step out into the air with my arms crossed over my chest, I jumped, without a second thought.

I plummeted deep down into the waterhole. I opened my eyes as I entered the water, a thunderous pounding noise, louder than the sound of waves under the sea, pulsated through my body. I could not see a thing; the water was thicker than the muddy waters in the dam at home. The current was pulling at me, getting stronger by the second, the buoyancy of the life vest lifting me up to the surface.

My head bobbed above the water, and our guide who was down on the level I was on yelled at me instantly with panic in his eyes. 'Move over to the side, there is a rope to hang onto.'

'I can't, the current is too strong,' I yelled back at him.

He could hardly hear me over the booming noise coming from the wall of water about to hit us. He was less than a metre away.

The guide reached his hand out to mine. I lunged my arm in his direction but the current was too strong. Our hands slipped by each other like ships passing in the night, and I was pulled under the water and swept away in a torrent of water so wild, so ferocious it looked like a frothy chocolate milkshake still in the blender.

Let your body go, don't fight it, I heard my inner voice say.

My mind immediately flashed back to being with my dad on the farm; I could hear his voice, all the times he had drummed into us as kids – 'Don't ever, ever, ever go into flood waters. You will never survive it. Water is stronger than all of us. If you ever accidentally get washed away, let your body go limp and hold your breath. You'll get pushed into branches and sticks and logs, and God knows what else. You've got more chance to stay alive if you just let go. Always let your body go, and always – above anything else – stay calm. Panic will only bring water into your lungs, and you will drown instantly. Stay calm.'

I held my breath.

I stayed calm.

My body and my mind went limp almost into a meditative state, focusing only on my survival, only on my breath. I knew nothing was going to win against Mother Nature's ferocity. I would never survive if I fought it. And if I tried to swim against it, I knew I would drown. No thoughts came into my mind, no emotion, no feeling of pain, no feeling of fear, nothing. I only concentrated on the sound of the pounding water crushing my ears, as it trashed itself violently against anything that was in its path. I surrendered to the waters and let myself get swept away.

It felt like an eternity.

The water ran fast.

Like a washing machine, with absolutely no control over my body, I was being tumbled down the gorge, arms and legs tossing brutally against the power of the water. Unable to see anything, I held my breath until I could grab a snippet of air when my face barely surfaced, before being pulled down under again into an underwater cyclone, with living beings trapped among its rage. Rumbling noises thumped in my ears.

Breathe.

Logs and branches flew turbulently at me, pounding my flesh. Multiple times I had the opportunity to grab mouthfuls of oxygen to keep me going until the next shove to the top, with only a nanosecond to get in as much air as I could, before my lungs would otherwise fill with water.

My lungs squeezed to capacity. *How long can I hold on?*

Another giant log, at least fifty centimetres in diameter rammed me in the stomach, with its force like that of a car slamming on its breaks, pushing me up and out of the water with my back against a boulder, crushing me. All I could feel was the air, the exquisite, pure, wondrous air replenishing my lungs. Air to breathe in and breathe out. Pushed up against the boulder at that moment, in that second, I had the chance now to really see what I was among.

There were rapids, so wild like Mother Nature was mad – what had we done to infuriate her? Was it even us? The noise of the tumultuous water pounded my ears and suffocated the canyon with its sound. I was unable to hear anything other than the giant waves crashing all around me.

Trying to orientate myself, I looked to my right and saw the lifeless bodies of my friends, face down, floating past me on top of the torrent.

I knew they had taken their last breath.

I looked straight ahead, back from where I had just come, to where I had been standing just moments before, among friends abuzz with anticipation of the adventures that lay ahead.

My friends were now dead.

Had it been minutes or seconds ago? I was no longer sure. The clear waters of moments before had now turned into an unrestrained effusion of mud-filled water. Giant waves rose up seemingly from nowhere within the water, flowing violently down the mountainside.

I looked to my left and saw a bank shrouded in natural green beauty, soft green leaves vibrated against the wild wind, moss covering every corner. The bank was not too far away, but far enough away that safety on the bank was out of reach. I would never make it.

At that moment, with the clean and crisp mountain air filling my lungs, I was trapped in the Saxetenbach Gorge between the majestic Swiss Alps. The clouds encircling their peaks had unleashed hell on us.

My senses were almost taken away from me at that moment, as I saw my life flash before me like a series of snapshots – where I had come from, what I had been through, but where was I headed? Did I have any control over where I went next?

I was in the middle of this torrent of destruction, with water hellishly lapping at my chin and mud covering my limbs, cramming underneath my fingernails and into my ears, coating my eyelids and eyelashes, and sliding up my nose as it pushed past me, with no escape.

The turbulent slurry filled with branches and large logs was rising higher by the second, whipping every inch of my body, swirling fiercely and blasting lightning bolts of pain through my skin as each log collided with me on its way down the mountainside. There was no stopping it.

Unable to scramble to the top of the boulder behind me, but momentarily spared from the coursing water by the log in front of me, I pondered how long I could wait for someone to possibly come and rescue me. Would anyone even come? Or would my hesitation end up with me being submerged by the rising waters or crushed by another log?

Or do I take charge of my own destiny? Do I go with my new-found friends, my new community of travel companions, unclear of what possibilities lay ahead? This new community of people, who despite our different histories, different lives and different experiences, offered no judgement of each other, just love and an acknowledgement of how curious life can be.

A community that accepted me – all of me.

Do I stay or do I go?

And with the thought of now, of being accepted, of belonging, of being me, and the thought of what had led me to this place, unable to see what was ahead of me . . . I let go.

Dragged underneath the avalanche of water and mud again, the ferocity of the water seemed to become even more intense as I flew down the rapids. The sound increased, blasting my ears with the pounding of the thrashing water. Holding onto my breath, I was starting to become strained. I could feel my body tensing; my ability to stay floppy and calm was beginning to fade. I couldn't hold my breath any longer – this was it. I had nothing left, not one millimetre of air. Was it my last breath? I couldn't hold on. With that thought, I prayed.

Please, dear Lord, dear Aunty Di, please don't let me die, because if I die, Mum won't cope.

With the end of my prayer, and no more ability to breathe, I drew my final breath.

Opening my mouth, I received another life-saving breath of air, as I was spontaneously lifted out of the raging rapids like someone pulling me out of the roaring brown thick, mud that surrounded me, pulling me out like a flying fish high above the water so that my chest was in mid-air. But there was no one there, just me and the ragging torrent. Was it my guardian angel? Was it Aunty Di? Was it God? I didn't know who it was, but I knew that I was being saved by something higher, something bigger than what I could understand.

And then I saw it.

The waterfall I was destined to go over.

'Oh, fuck,' I said out loud, and was dragged under again.

Spanning twenty metres across and the same going down, I was sucked under again, the sudden acceleration that proceeded a moment of near freefall over the edge of the waterfall.

And then . . .

I came up for air, surrounded by pristine, clear, dark black water like a loch. I was in a little alcove. I could see the bank, and looking up I saw three others lying on the bank. They were alive. With every ounce of my being, I desperately tried to move my body to swim to the water's edge. However, the more I tried to move, the more I remained stuck in one space. My body was entirely depleted; I couldn't move at all. The life vest was the only thing keeping me above the water.

I had been a champion swimmer as a child, and if ever I needed to swim, now was the time. I found strength from deep within my soul, a strength I knew I could rely on. Like in a slow-motion movie, I made my way over to the edge, slowly with every breath pounding in my chest, with only my arms pulling me through the water, the only part of my body that could move, that would move. I didn't think I would make it. Had it not been for the life vest, I would have drowned in the depths of the ravine. I had nothing left in me.

Reaching up to the edge, I grabbed onto the grass, but it slipped through my fingers, and I slid back down into the water only to bob back up from my life vest. I gasped for breath, for life, trying to lift myself up again, only to find that now I was unable to grab the grass. I bobbed up and down in the water, desperate to get out, but I couldn't, no matter how hard I tried. My body was incapable of moving. I was frozen solid.

A pair of feet stood before me and then hands reached down to my shoulders, trying to pull me ashore by my life vest, but I was stuck and then a long stick was rammed into my chest, sticking out of my life vest through both sides of my armholes. I wiggled back down into the water to try to free it, terrified of being swept away again. Adrenaline started to surge through me. I pulled the stick free.

'Go!' I yelled at the pair of feet.

I was quickly yanked up onto the grass.

Safe.

I lay there panting, legs still in the water, half of my body lying on the wet ground.

'Thank you,' I whispered.

'No worries,' was the reply.

I looked up as tears filled my eyes. It was one of the beer guys from my bus. 'You're alive! You're safe!' I whispered. A rush of emotion ran over me.

Looking around, I saw two others also lying on the bank. One guy who I didn't know was screaming in pain and grabbing his leg, it looked broken. I almost couldn't hear him or see him from too much mud in my eyes, stuck to my eyelids and between my eyelashes. I tried to blink, to clear them, but there was just too much. I had no energy to wipe my eyes. I stared, half blind. He sounded like a dull buzzing noise beneath the crashing sound of the floodwaters only a few metres from where we lay. Unable to move, unable to think, unable to help anyone, I lay there, motionless, barley alive.

A voice appeared from further up the mound beside the waterfall.

'Come with me; I'll lead you to safety,' a man called out as he approached us. He was on foot and had just climbed over part of the mountain by the edge of the canyon.

Suddenly I got to my feet and started barking instructions to everyone. Adrenaline kicked in. I felt nothing, only the impulse to get to safety. It was all that mattered. My life was worth something; it was worth more. I was more. I knew it. I chose life. My body was now moving with enough force to push twenty cars in one swift movement.

I charged ahead.

'Quick, we need to move before it comes and gets us again. Come on; we need to move it and get to higher ground!' Like an army soldier in combat, I moved my broken body and followed the stranger up the mountainside, along with the others who had ended up in the same place as me. The rain was pouring down, adding to the mud that our feet were sliding in as we made our way back up the side of the mountain. Mud was slipping between my toes, my wetsuit shoes were no longer on my feet. The mountain was so steep it was almost unclimbable and the slope had become like a mini mudslide heading back towards the rapids below us. Holding onto every tree with arms scavenging for a spot to grab onto to pull ourselves up, gasping for breath, almost crawling, we made our way up towards the safety of the road.

'Look at that,' someone said. 'Look at what we have just been through.'

We all turned around and looked down, back into the canyon. There were no more bodies floating in front of us, just the torrent of white water that flooded the canyon and the mud sliding down the side of the mountain filled with more debris, adding to the destruction below us.

'I don't want to look at it,' I said, 'it might keep rising, come on, we need to get to higher ground.' I sped up again, climbing the side of the mountain as quickly as I could. My fight or flight mode had kicked in. I chose survival. I no longer walked – I was fleeing for safety.

We reached the road where we had first begun our journey on the mountain. The stranger who had led us up to the side of the mountain reached down to pull me up over the mound that was the edge of the road, it was stopping us from our final step to safety. Grabbing his hand, we connected. I looked up and saw that the stranger was my guide whose hand had slipped past mine.

'You've survived,' he said embracing me. 'I thought I lost you. I couldn't grab you.' Sobbing, he held me, like a long-lost relative.

Relief flooded through me as we cried in each other's arms.

Stopping abruptly, realising that there were others, still unaccounted for, we needed to move, and fast.

'Let's go for help,' I said as the fierce sound of helicopters hovering above echoed up the canyon in time with the thunder. I looked up to the sky and saw multiple helicopters with long ropes hanging off them.

'Let's get to base. I'll see what's happening,' the guide said.

In my mind I wanted to run away from the canyon faster than an Olympic sprinter, run to safety, run to anywhere else. But my body was weak and tortured and wasn't capable of moving at even a hare's pace – it was more like a snail's pace. My adrenaline rush had started to subside now that I had reached safety.

We walked along in silence, still numb from what had happened – no one said a word.

The distant bellows of a current raging below us vibrated all around. The crunching sound of leaves beneath my feet soothed my tired lungs. I was no longer fighting for air. I could breathe. Still hearing the rampaging water down in the canyon, I didn't look back.

In the distance we saw the same minibus that we came up in, but now it was further down the mountain, as someone had come and collected it. Guides were rushing around; orders were barked at each other – ropes, cables. It was the scene of a rescue attempt.

But they were too late.

I already knew that.

Chapter 21

FROM CLEAR TO DARK

Our guide told us to stay together, and then he went over to a group of rescuers to find out what was going on. He came back to us and informed us that we would be taken to the local hospital and that he would be staying on to help with the rescue mission. I could do nothing else but take his advice. I wasn't prepared or equipped with anything to help anyone else – my body and mind had become vacant.

We all climbed into the bus, the engine started, and we travelled back down the mountain; although this time, the bus was almost empty.

Still no one spoke.

We pulled into the driveway at the hospital. Four wheelchairs were waiting for us, which we climbed into gingerly, and then we were pushed in through the hospital with its white walls and gleaming lights. The lights were blinding in contrast to the darkness of the forest. No fresh air surrounded us anymore; the only smell was of disinfectant.

We were all put into a room and told to wait until others arrived. The room had one bed in it pushed up against a wall, and at the other end of the room there was a long skinny rectangular window just below the ceiling that looked out onto soil, roots and the base of plants growing; they looked like a type of giant grass.

It became apparent that we were in a room that was underground. Still, no one spoke.

I could hear helicopters coming. Closer and closer they seemed. We could see snippets of the outside world though the window; the grass leaves rustled wildly with the dirt flying about like a tornado as the helicopter landed. After a short time, it went again. The leaves stopped rustling; all was quiet once more.

'I wonder who they'll bring in next?' said one of the other survivors.

The nurse came and spoke to all of us in English with a strong Swiss accent. 'There has been an accident. It will be all over the news. You must all ring your families and tell them that you are safe,' she announced without any compassion or emotion.

Is this just how Swiss people deal with tragedy? 'You mean in the news in Switzerland, or the news in our countries?' I asked.

'It will be in the news around the world. You have a five-minute time limit, as all calls are international. Follow me,' the nurse said, pointing to me. 'I will come back for each of you, one by one.'

I got up and stumbled slightly, then followed the nurse to a tiny phone booth.

'You have five minutes,' she said again and walked away.

I dialled the number for home. I had no idea what the time was back home; I had no idea what the time was here. The phone rang three times. Dad answered.

'Hi Dad,' I said.

'Hello possum, what's happened?' he replied

'Is it in the news already? They're all dead; I'm alright,' I said, stunned that it was already making headlines – hell, I didn't even know the extent of what had happened yet.

'No possum, it's two in the morning, but something must have happened for you to be ringing at this hour. What's happened?' Dad asked.

'Listen Dad, I don't have long, as there are a bunch of us needing to make calls. There's been a big accident, and I'm in hospital in Switzerland,' I replied, unable to give any more information than the bare basics.

'Two minutes!' I heard the nurse calling out to me.

'They told us to ring you and let you know that I'm okay. You're going to see this all over the news tomorrow, Dad.'

'Okay, possum,' he said, 'listen, your mother wants to talk to you.'

The nurse was now coming towards me and tapping her wrist, indicating that time was up.

'Tiffy, are you okay, darling?' Mum asked.

'Yes Mum, I'm fine. Mum, I've been in a big accident. I'm in hospital in Switzerland. I'll let you know what's going on, as soon as I know more details. I've got to go. I love you. I'm okay. Bye.' I hung up the phone.

The nurse walked me back to the room and took everyone individually to make precious phone calls back home.

And then we waited.

More helicopters came. More grass rustled by the window. But no one else ever arrived.

Hours seemed to go by before we were seen to. And then all of a sudden doctors and nurses came barging in through the solid wooden door. It creaked as it opened, the only other noise other than the sound of helicopters that I'd heard in hours.

One by one we were taken for examinations, X-rays and treatments. On my initial examination, the Swiss doctors found nothing wrong with me, I just had some bruising, and they said that I would be fine. A hospital gown was distributed, along with soap, towels and directions to the showers. I wasn't sure what was worse, a hospital gown or my filthy wetsuit covered in mud, or being in unexplained pain. I welcomed a hot shower; the water ran brown as the debris started melting off my skin. I had mud everywhere – up my nose, in my mouth, under my eyelids – it was in places I didn't know mud could go.

I placed my clothes in a plastic bag. Bending down was almost unbearable.

I hurt.

I looked in the mirror, in-between my eyelashes were little tiny pieces of mud, I rewashed my face, and more brown water ran down the sink. I blew my nose, more mud. I just couldn't seem to get rid of it.

The nurse waited outside for me. I handed her my plastic bag and collapsed into the wheelchair, grateful for the relief of sitting down. We scooted through the hospital like mice, unnoticed by anyone through back passageways and long, dimly lit hallways, wheeled into service lifts, along empty corridors, ultimately arriving in our own private ward.

There was not another patient in sight.

The crisp, white linen on the bed was icy cold as I slowly and carefully slid between the sheets, feeling a sense of ease as I rested my head against the pillow. The air was cold and fresh, a welcome change for my lungs, but they still hurt.

Maybe the pain I feel is just shock? We're all suffering shock. When will the rest of us be back here in the ward?

I waited, closing my eyes, but sleep wouldn't come. I started shivering and shaking uncontrollably, as shock stated to sink in. The air felt cold against my face with the sheets cold on my body. I pulled the thin cotton blanket up closer to my neck to try to get warm.

Looking over to a large window with the curtains drawn closed, I wondered if we could open the curtains to see outside. I tried to move, but was incapable. I decided I could open the curtains later. Better to rest now while waiting for everyone else to arrive.

The nurse came in with a tray of food.

'Would you mind opening the curtains please? I'd love to be able to see some natural light. I tried to get up, but it was a bit hard,' I asked the nurse.

'I'm so sorry, miss, you can't open the curtain, and nor can I,' replied the nurse. 'Hospital staff have been advised by the police and International Affairs to keep you in a secure facility. The grounds of the hospital are crawling with paparazzi, they don't know where you all are, and we need to keep it that way.'

Paparazzi! What on earth are the paparazzi here for? What the hell is going on and where is everyone else?

Too tired to ask questions, too weak to make a sound, I just lay there with my mind racing.

One by one the remaining five of us from our tiny room in emergency arrived, all in hospital gowns, washed and showered and now fed. Everyone asked each other if anyone knew any information. But we were all the same – clueless as to what had happened.

It felt like we had been in the ward for hours, all of us drifting in and out of restless sleep. The only sound I could hear was of the air-conditioning being pumped through the hospital – it was starting to hum to me, like the sound of the engine on the bus.

Finally, footsteps sounded up the corridor, after what felt like more hours, and another nurse arrived. 'You have some friends to visit,' she announced.

More footsteps. Then friends came bellowing through the doors to the ward.

Everyone had someone to visit them – everyone except me.

I was alone – again.

It was the most alone I had ever felt throughout my entire trip.

Hearing the cries of joy and of sadness erupt from the others, desperation filled my soul. I looked straight ahead, unable to look at anyone else. Silent tears flowed down my cheeks. All I needed was someone to wrap their arms around me and say everything was okay, or not even say anything, just wrap me in their comforting embrace.

But I had nothing. I had no one.

I was alone.

I watched everyone talking about what was happening, what was suspected, what had actually happened, but no one spoke to me. I was invisible to every single person in the room.

After everything I had been through with all the years I'd spent on my own, pondering life, and being in my peaceful place on our farm, moving out of home so young, living in a nightmare relationship and keeping all my secrets safe, I had never experienced such loneliness. It was pure loneliness that surged in the pit of my stomach, filling it with a thick, black hole and bringing me . . . nothing. My chest hurt with the heartache of lonesomeness.

I felt despair rising inside me as my tears continued to fall down my face silently.

More footsteps sounded, I waited to see the nurse, but looking up I saw Cassandra come around the corner, running to my side.

I began to sob uncontrollably at the sight of her, and every part of my body ached as my lonesomeness lifted – I was truly no longer alone.

✷ ✷ ✷

Doctors, nursing staff and our visitors were bustling around the ward. We slowly started piecing together snippets of limited information that we had – who had returned to the chalet, and who had not. Though still, no one told us what had happened.

The realisation that the six of us were the only survivors, out of the forty-five participants and eight guides, who were in the water at the time the flood hit, started to slowly sink in

We were all young adventurers seeking life experiences that we could hold onto for years to come, but soon we discovered that twenty-one of those beautiful young people would never have the opportunity to remember those adventures, as eighteen tourists were swept away to their deaths that fateful day. Eight brave guides continued to attempt a rescue mission that was destined to fail, and the flood took the lives of three guides with it.

Twenty-one participants sat on the banks of the canyon watching the death and destruction of the torrent that raged past them, watching on as their friends, family and travel companions were swept away.

Cousins, friends, lovers and loved ones from afar would now never get to experience life's wonders or a family of their own, or the ups and downs of daily life that throws curve balls at you any chance it gets. Wonder and magic, pain and loss, joy and sadness, none of these feelings would they ever experience again. An opportunity to grow old and become wise from life's lessons – all of this was stolen from them.

None of us were fully aware of the reality of what was actually going on, or the impact that this event would have on our lives and on so many others. Like mushrooms, we were still in the dark. We just knew at that time that the six of us were in hospital. There was no news on where the others were, but I knew where they were.

I had seen them, floating face down in the canyon. None of them had come through that heavy wooden door into our room. Not one more person was brought to us in the hospital, and they wouldn't be, because they were dead. Everyone else hung onto hope. There had been no official news from anyone. Maybe they were having surgery or they had been taken someplace else, another hospital perhaps? But I knew the truth; I just couldn't bring myself to say the words out loud.

I sat there quietly, not saying a word to anyone and looked down at my bed. My legs had started to swell by now and were about double the size. My pain was intensifying; I was struggling to breathe, anxiety filling every pore. I was cold and clammy and started to feel faint. How could I tell them what I was feeling? Would they even believe me? I didn't know who to speak too or what to say.

I thought I might throw up.

Cassandra ran to get the nurse; she could see I was fading fast.

'Time for you all to leave now. They have been through enough for one day, time for some rest,' the nurse said as she entered the room.

Cassandra embraced me. I grunted in pain, as the hug was unbearably painful. I was unable to raise my arms to return the hug.

'See you soon,' she said and kissed the top of my forehead.

'She needs pain relief,' Cassandra said to the nurse as she walked out of the room waving.

Resting my head back down on the pillow, I closed my eyes and finally fell asleep, drifting in and out of nightmares.

Chapter 22

UNCHARTED TERRITORY

Day one after the accident.

After breakfast in the hospital, we were transferred back to our chalet, still numb and in the dark as to what had happened or what we were about to face. We were all placed in wheelchairs and wheeled back to the same place we entered. News cars, journalists with microphones and cameras were all waiting out on the streets.

And even though the team taking care of us thought they had a well thought-out plan in order to get us to the minibus, assuming that we could remain anonymous, the plan failed.

As soon as we were out of the safety of the hospital grounds, cars were following us, police lights were flashing, and journalists in vehicles were racing up behind us trying to get a picture of us. We had been instructed to put our heads down and cover ourselves, so no one could see us. We had no idea of what was happening; we had been sheltered from the media thus far during our stay in hospital, and no one had told us what was going on outside the building, and now we had been thrown into the streets like scraps to vultures, and we could not escape.

We finally arrived at our chalet, which was surrounded by police tape and a police guard.

What on earth is that for?

And then I saw them.

There was a media frenzy with over 200 journalists from around the globe standing along the boundary of the police tape. Lights were flashing, cameras were zooming – the journalists were desperately waiting for someone, anyone to give them something to report to the world.

Our fellow travellers, eager to see who was on the bus, and who was coming back to them, raced towards the bus. Still no one had been given any information about what had happened and where everyone else was.

I hobbled down the steps of the bus, hardly able to move.

Cassandra pushed her way through the crowd to help me. 'You okay?' she asked.

The sounds of people gasping, crying and rejoicing, along with the snapping of camera shutters as the media viciously tried to capture each moment, filled my ears; I was so overwhelmed. I could hardly make any sense out of what was happening. I nodded at Cassandra, still unable to say a word, like someone had taken my voice box away – nothing would come out.

People I didn't even know were running up to me, saying, 'Oh you're alive! You're alive!'

I felt bamboozled as I looked out to a sea of faces and could feel terror race throughout me. I needed to get out of there.

Kimberly came running down the stairs in a flood of tears. Relief washed over me at the sight of another member of my tribe.

'I tried to come to the hospital, I tried, but there was no room, there was no room,' she kept saying between sobs and hugging me for dear life.

I screamed out in pain.

She let go instantly. 'Oh, I'm sorry, where does it hurt? Come on, let's get you inside,' Kimberly said as she put her arms around me and helped me back through the crowd and into the chalet.

With my tribe by my side, supporting me and lifting me up, I made my way to the chalet, still in a daze and still so confused. They tried to move me quickly; I couldn't walk quickly, I couldn't do anything quickly.

The police were waiting for us as we entered the mess hall, about to deliver the news that I already knew from witnessing it with my own eyes.

Police then announced the tragedy to us, confirming twenty-one fatalities from Australia, New Zealand, South Africa, England and Switzerland; they included eighteen tourists and three guides. They were now waiting for the confirmation of identification, which would happen over the next few days. Authorities had contacted all families of the deceased, and an investigation into the incident was underway.

At this stage, the police were aware of the fact that there appeared to have been a flash flood down the Saxetenbach Gorge at approximately 6 pm on 27 July 1999. The police continued to inform us that there had been great interest in the incident from many international news reporters and they had made camp outside of the temporary boundary put in place.

Wails of tears, screams, and shouts vibrated within the four walls of the mess hall.

I just stood there, frozen still.

The police suspected that there would be more concrete information in the days to come.

'We advise that all of you must stay indoors and not engage with the media until we have further information. Also, as this is now under police investigation, you may not leave the chalet until further notice,' one of the police officers declared.

We were hostages.

I left the hall, not wanting to be with anyone, and slowly wandered back to my room. The same room where one night ago I had been playing the chocolate game with all my new friends, sitting in a circle, being childish and having fun, without a care in the world.

I looked out the window to the sea of journalists. Tents went up and sleeping bags pulled out. It seemed like they were settling in. Questions filled my mind. *Why do the journalists have to be loitering outside our chalet? Now I can't even go outside. Not that I can really walk. I am so, so sore. How long will the police investigations go? How long can an inquiry in Switzerland last? What does this all mean? Will there be a court hearing? Will I have to give evidence? What will happen if I go outside? How will the media react? Perhaps I need to stay under the radar?*

I was too sore to be involved in anything. I tried to take deep breaths, but every single second was a struggle. I closed the curtains abruptly in annoyance.

Slowly sitting down on my bed, I noticed my daypack still sitting on it from the day before and my packet of Swiss army knives sitting next to it, which Cassandra must have put there. Touching the green fabric of my daypack, feeling its rough surface, I saw the stains from where I'd spilt drinks on it in Paris and Rome. I'd seen so much, in such a short period and now . . . and now . . .

My mind went still.

Opening the zipper to my pack and hearing the familiar sound, I found my journal. Flicking through the pages, I saw all the memories I'd made. I didn't know if I could finish this chapter, keep travelling, or deal with what came next. I was too sore to think straight. Breathing was getting harder and harder, taking every ounce of effort to get some air into my body.

I noticed in the back of my journal some writing paper that I'd forgotten I'd packed – for just in case I needed to write a letter.

I needed to write a letter, immediately.

With pen to paper, I started writing to my saving grace, Cassandra.

To My Dear Friend Cassandra,

What a lucky girl I am to have a friend like you.
Your strength and compassion shine through; I

know a lot of people would not have been able to cope without your strength and courage. To know that you care so deeply brought tears to my eyes. Although we have only been friends for a short while, I feel that I know you so well. I will always remember you and our wonderful holiday – up until this tragedy. I want you to know that I'll always be a friend when you're in need of one.

My love always,

Tiff x

Leaving the note on her pillow, I wrapped myself in my sleeping bag and tried to get some rest.

* * *

I woke up. The lights were out, and the curtains were still drawn. I could hear the soft murmur of my roommates sleeping. I tried to move but my body wouldn't. I tried to roll over, no, couldn't do that. I tried the other side, no, couldn't do that side either. I tried sitting up, no, couldn't do that. I couldn't move. I was so desperately thirsty. *How am I going to get a drink?*

I kept trying to move, but nothing would budge. I lay there panting, exhausted from trying to get a glass of water. Desperate for hydration, I tried again.

Come on, Tiffany. You can do this. I said to myself, hoping my own words of encouragement would make a difference.

Grunting, I tried to sit up. Nope, still lying down.

This was a problem.

Rustling sounds came from above my bed. *Oh dear, I must be making too much noise trying to move, I'm waking people up,* I thought, feeling frustrated.

A tiny creak from the wooden bed and movement from the top bunk sounded, when feet appeared.

Damn it. I've woken up Cassandra. I don't want to wake up anyone.

'Are you okay?' she asked as she knelt down next to my bed.

Still paralysed, I slowly tried to turn my head.

'I heard you grunting, and I thought you might have been having a nightmare. I just came down to check that you're okay.'

'I'm desperate for a glass of water, and I can't seem to move,' I replied.

With gentle hands, she slowly lifted my head up and brought a glass of water with a straw in it to my lips; the refreshing liquid replenished my thirst.

My head back down, still trying to breathe, I said gratefully, 'Thank you.'

'No, thank you, for the note. You are the kindest person I have ever met; I'm so pleased that you are my friend,' she said, stroking my hair. She sat there for ages without saying a word as I slowly drifted back to sleep, no longer alone.

✻ ✻ ✻

Day two after the accident.

Time moved slowly – the hours felt like days, the days felt like months – having our freedom taken away from us only made it worse.

Everyone needed support in some form, either from family and friends back home or those around them. Test line phones were brought in by Swiss Authorities, enabling us to have a secure line to talk to our loved ones across the sea, but only for three minutes, for security reasons – it was barely enough time to say hello. Voices echoed around the giant room, as we were all squished together in what was once our dining hall, which was now a call centre.

I found it harder and harder to walk. The pain in my body had started to increase, and as a consequence, my strength slowly declined. My friends lifted me up at every turn, even to help me walk, becoming my human crutches.

To dull the pain, I slept. Investigations were underway, and still I slept. Interviews commenced as authorities were having trouble with the identification process of the fatalities, as the majority of the bodies were international. There were no records or information on any of the individuals. Eight brave people from both coach parties volunteered to pre-identify the bodies, this ensuring that when the families arrived, they would be directed to their own family member. Jo and Cassandra were two of those courageous individuals.

With police coming and going, statements being made, identifications underway and media continually loitering around the chalet, it seemed impossible to do anything at all. Although to me, it didn't impact me as much – I just kept sleeping.

Eventually, I was allowed to make an escape trip to the doctors in Winderswill to get crutches and a brace for my 'bruised' ribs, as the hospital had said. The doctors felt that they didn't need to do further tests, as the hospital had done X-rays and no broken bones showed up.

But I certainly felt like I was broken somewhere, and I couldn't understand how I could have just been bruised and battered – the pain I was feeling was excruciating. But they were the doctors, so they should have known, I presumed.

And while my body, mind and spirit had become numb with the intensity of the pain and the trauma, I didn't know what else to do or what else to say to anyone, including my family. I soldiered on, just like everyone tried to, as best as I could. But the pain was almost to the point of no return, both physically and emotionally.

I spoke to my parents daily, assuring them that I was okay, in my three-minute conversations. I told them that I was only suffering from some bruising, just as the doctors had said. What else could I say? Even though it was the worst bruise pain I had ever felt, I didn't let them know that. I didn't let anyone know that. How could I complain? I was alive. I just told them what the doctor and the hospital had told me; there was nothing to worry about.

The pressure to have my family come to Switzerland was amounting to heights I could not withstand. Mum and Dad both wanted to come and take care of me, but I couldn't handle dealing with extra people, not even those I loved. I was barely coping with myself. We had no idea how long we would be kept as hostages while the investigations were ramped up.

I didn't mind so much – if I stayed in the chalet, at least I was with my tribe and I was still near those that were lost. I felt closer to them if I stayed in the chalet, and to myself. I wondered if their souls were still lingering around us? *Will they find their way back home, or will they stay here for all of eternity?* I didn't know where else I wanted to be. All I knew was that for now, I just needed to be in the chalet, near them.

Daily briefings from the police made it impossible to feel like anything was going back to normal. Part of the police investigations included individual police reports with added police briefings, along with the pre-identification of the bodies.

And then finally the police assured us that the opportunity to leave and go home was getting close, maybe within the next few days. But I wasn't sure how I felt about that.

The Australian Government was working tirelessly with the families involved and assured my parents that I would be arriving home soon, and if they flew over to me, we may, in fact, miss each other mid flight. I insisted they stay home and wait for me. I would get the next flight back to Sydney, whenever that would be, as soon as possible.

Hard as it was for them to stay away, they did, but it was even harder to keep the media at bay, as they bombarded my family home. Television vans parked out the front of our farm, and journalists were phoning the house at all hours and asking for my story. My family constantly gave a firm 'no', going into protection mode, while they waited for my arrival, filled with nothing but worry and anxiety. They were desperate for me to be back in their arms.

The air in the chalet had become stale with the overflowing emotion and weight that everyone carried. The sooner we could get out of there the better it would be for everyone. But I didn't know if I could leave, though I didn't have a choice. I felt trapped in so many ways.

There were no more sounds of laughter filling the halls, as the sounds of sobbing had replaced them. Some people were angry; some people were quiet; some people were sad and cried a lot. Everyone was grieving in different ways; we were walking in unchartered territory, every single one of us.

I became one of the quiet ones. I kept to myself most of the time. My physical pain and my state of mind blended together – I felt numb. My injuries remained unidentified; I had no pain relief of any sort. It hurt too much physically to talk to anyone, and I hadn't even started to process my emotional state. I began to feel angry – angry that the accident had happened, angry that we were stuck in Switzerland, angry that we couldn't finish the trip, angry that those whom we had lost couldn't finish their journeys, finish their lives. I could feel the anger like poison spreading through my veins. So I chose to hide any sort of emotion and time became a blur.

Cassandra had become my protector throughout those days. If at some point someone came into our room to ask me questions about what had happened, she would quickly shoo them away. For this I was thankful. Even though we had all been together now for nearly a month, and our bond had grown stronger, we needed more space than what this place of dark timber cladding that was holding us all prisoner could provide. The pretty white and red flowers on the windowsills and picturesque Swiss Alps towering intensely over us no longer brought comfort. A waterfall was in clear view in the near distance, cascading gracefully onto the earth. I found I could no longer look at it.

The media continued to camp on the boundaries of the chalet; they were relentless. I soon found out what the media would do if we did go outside for a tiny, limping walk. Without leaving the grounds of the property, with crutches beneath my armpits and Kimberly and Cassandra holding me up, the media pounded us with questions, cameras flashing, and voices calling.

My body started shaking. I wanted to scream at them, to make them go away. To make it all go away.

'Just keep walking, ignore them,' Kimberly said as she grabbed my arm just that bit tighter.

'Let's not walk around that side of the building again,' Cassandra said as she helped place me on to a log.

I could hardly breathe. I was exhausted and I'd only walked twenty metres.

The sound of the journalists had died down. We were now alone again, in a secluded part of the garden at the back of the chalet, underneath an enormous elm tree – the perfect spot for resting and admiring the view of the formidable Alps.

The three of us sat on the log together. We stared up into the sheer cliff faces of the mountains, listening only to the leaves rustling above us from the breeze that was blowing our way.

'Do you think they can see us?' Kimberly asked, tears streaming down her face. 'Do you think they are still up there, watching everything happening to us down here?'

We sat there for what seemed like an eternity, holding each other's hand.

I'd started to moan uncontrollably with the discomfort from my body and pain in my heart.

'Come on; let's get you back inside,' Cassandra said, reaching down for me again.

As they lifted me up, I groaned with every movement.

Entering back into the chalet, I could feel that the energy was continuing to plummet, as people were getting more agitated by the hour. The staff had closed the bar since the accident, terrified of what could happen if anyone started drinking.

Contiki staff continued to feed us, support us as best they could, but they needed help too – we all needed help. And then from out of nowhere – like magic – counsellors were made available to us all, specialising in trauma. Most people chose to talk about what was happening, but I wasn't interested. I didn't want to tell anyone what I had seen, what I had felt, how my body felt and just how much it hurt. How could I? The more I thought about it, the more it pained me inside and out.

A memorial service was arranged for us with a local priest. The sun shone down on us as it commenced that afternoon. Sitting in a circle made up of logs, the Alps loomed down on us, and the waterfall in the distance pounded against the boulders and rocks. I could almost hear IT again – the water.

I closed my eyes and prayed for God to make it stop. When I opened them again, I felt immediate relief wash over me. I was safe – for now.

During the service, people were given the opportunity to say a few words, providing some of us with some type of closure, or something. I wasn't sure. I felt anger still, part of my grief I guessed. I wasn't angry at anyone in particular, just at everything, like the world was trying to break me. I sat there looking at everyone and noticed our missing companions. Flashbacks came to me, and unable to stop them, I kept blinking and grabbing my own wrists and twisting them, to let myself know that I was alive, in the present moment, and not in the water again. The service was lovely and highly appropriate. But all I could see were my friends, floating.

Lying in bed that night – now propped up on cushions, which Cassandra had arranged for me so that I might be more comfortable, with a drink bottle and a long straw next to my bed – I pondered my situation and what was going to happen next. I couldn't stay there forever; I'd go mad if I did. Or was I already going mad? I wasn't sure.

The longer I stayed in Switzerland, the longer I was overseas, the longer I could work on finding me – but hadn't I already found myself? Just before the accident?

And now . . . and now?

It felt like it had all been taken away from me. Everything had been taken away from me. I felt so many mixed emotions. Anger – why had this happened? Guilt – why had I survived? Joy – I had survived. Grief – I had lost friends. Pain – in my body and in my heart.

The pain was constant. With every breath came a reminder of what had happened. Excruciating pain beat into my chest like a knife stabbing me every second – my ribs were not healing from the bruising. I felt pain with every step, my legs had blown up like balloons and were almost unable to be moved. I felt pain with every mouthful of food, as my jaw was unable to close properly. I felt pain in my stomach from where the log had rammed me.

My vortex of emotion consumed my every breath, and I realised that I now no longer felt shame. I no longer felt hurt. I no longer felt violated, or unappreciated, or disrespected, or worth nothing, or useless, or scared, or needing someone else to make me feel something. I now felt truly whole – the good, the bad, the horrendous and the joy, all together, all making up every single part of me.

I had been through the worst of it; I came out the other side. I had survived.

And now I had the pondering questions that I'd had all those years ago. *What is my purpose?* I knew that I was destined to do something more. Was this why I had been spared? I could see no other reason for it. I now needed to find what that was and make it happen. Make it a reality to be the me that I was destined to be. But first I needed to heal. And to do that, I had to listen to myself.

With these thoughts, the reality of going home was at the forefront of my mind. I needed help recovering; I needed the strength of my family to help me make it through the next phase. This meant no skydiving out of London, or jobs with friends and living in the United Kingdom or further abroad. I knew I couldn't do any of it. Maybe I wasn't meant to.

I had to go home.

With this reality came a heavy sigh, filled with courage, anguish and an inner strength that was building inside me. I knew I could move forward from a past of hurt, pain and suffering. For I now had a different hurt, pain and suffering. I had more challenges to face than ever before, but I also had more determination and a renewed sense of self-worth, something I was not prepared to let go of, under any circumstance. I was broken in so many ways, and the only thing left for me to do was glue myself back together.

And for this to happen, I needed my home.

I needed my special place, where it all began.

Chapter 23

HOME

Day three after the accident.

A great sigh of relief echoed out through the mess hall as the chalet staff gave us all the news we were longing to hear – we could go home! Today! Contiki would get us all back to London if we chose, and would then assist with getting us back to our home countries. Some travellers decided to stay behind.

Cassandra and I knew that the gale force winds of life, which had seemed to blow in both of our directions, were still following us as we had travelled throughout Europe. But now that we had each other as kindred spirits, we could go forward, together, no matter where we were, no matter where the wind pushed us, no matter if we were together or apart. We were lifelong friends now. Cassandra chose to stay; I decided to head back to London and make my way home.

Everyone clambered onto the bus solemnly – heads down, no one said a word. I was the last to get on. Cassandra helped me. I no longer had my crutches (I had to leave them behind), nor my shoes, as they no longer fitted me because my feet had swollen so much, not even my thongs fit. Andrea and Kimberly, who were also heading back to London, reached down to help me get aboard. After a long goodbye and an exchange of phone numbers and emails, we left Switzerland behind.

I found a seat on my own. There were plenty of spare seats now. The bus was quiet. It was the first time we had been aboard the bus and moving to our next destination without our tour song.

Placing my head against the windowpane, I felt unable to deal with anything that was happening. How did people survive through this kind of grief? I was incapable of feeling anymore, seeing anymore, being anymore or doing anymore. The pain burning into my body was worse than what I imagined childbirth would be. The only way I could deal with it was to sleep again. It was the only tool I had.

Travelling back to London from Bern turned into a thick blanket of fog I couldn't see through. I felt like I was a walking zombie. Kimberly was taking charge of where I needed to go and what I needed to do. She found me wheelchairs at the airport, so I didn't have to walk so far, especially without my shoes on. She had taken over the protector role from Cassandra.

And then there we were, back in the same hotel room as the night I got into London the night before this trip began. Though this time, I was sharing it with my new tribe. It was the same bedspreads, same bathroom, same everything. Except that I wasn't the same. Everything about me was different. Everything about all of us was different. Nothing within us would ever be the same again.

On our last night together, the remnants of our tour group decided to head out for dinner. There weren't many of us left; most people had gone their own way as soon as they hit London, and some went home straight from Bern. Unable to cope with what had happened, grief-stricken and needing their own family and friends, their own time to heal, they moved on quickly.

I looked at my bag, unable to bend down and pick it up, unable to find my clothes or pull things out of my bag, unable to move. My body had now swollen up like a balloon. None of my clothes fit anymore, except for the pants Mum had made me, with their comfortable elastic waist, which were a blessing. But I couldn't wear them out for dinner, as I'd been wearing them since the accident, and I had to wear them on the plane tomorrow.

Kimberly reached into my bag and pulled out my pink dress from Spain. 'How about this one? It's nice and stretchy?' she asked. 'Plus, it looks great on you, and you won't be able to see your rib brace or anything with it on.'

She was a lifesaver.

I looked at myself as I put my make-up on, trying to hide the swelling and bruising on my face. I saw another version of me. I looked older, different, and somehow, even with everything that my body was going through, I looked better than when I looked in the mirror back home, when I saw myself living a shell of a life.

This was anything but a shell of a life.

There I was, in London, living through I didn't know exactly what, but it was something, and it was big, and it was all about to end, tomorrow. I felt another pang of anger. I shook my head, no anger tonight. *Tonight, we celebrate life.*

It was an early night for me; sitting was too painful. Kimberly took me back to the room. Hugs and tears flowed as we said our goodbyes. Tomorrow we would all be making our own way towards the next chapter of this life.

What I wanted more than anything was to stay with my new friends – friends who understood what was going on, what I was feeling, what we were all feeling. But I knew I couldn't. As much as I needed my new friends, I needed my family more. They were the ones who would take care of me, nurture me, and get me back on my feet. I had to go home. I just wasn't quite ready for it yet.

I wasn't able to think about how I would manage at home or what I would do next. All I could think about was my next breath and if I took a shallow enough breath then maybe it wouldn't hurt so much. The pain was still constant in my chest. How could I ever explain to anyone what I was going through? I knew no one back home could ever understand what it felt like to lose them, all twenty-one of them, in something so horrific, something so tragic – something that I was a part of. It all seemed so huge, almost like watching myself in a movie, where I was one of the lead roles. How could I ever explain any of it to my family? My family didn't even know who these people were.

I felt trapped knowing I had to go home. How could I say 'hello' to my family when all I wanted to do was not say goodbye to my friends. I wasn't ready to leave them – leaving Cassandra was hard enough. We were together in this, even though we were all so different and dealt with the tragedy in so many different ways. I finally felt like I belonged somewhere. And now it was all being taken away from me.

✳ ✳ ✳

Day five after the accident.

My anger grew. Walking on board the plane, I still had no shoes on, as now my feet were black and blue from the bruising and soft tissue damage. I could feel my body tensing at the thought of being on home soil, and still I had no pain relief for my 'bruising'.

I was travelling home with some of the other survivors. I could feel my anger burning up inside me. *Are they angry too?* I didn't know. I could barely speak to ask them; speaking was difficult, the pain in my jaw was preventing me from too much chitchat.

All I knew was that I was still in enormous amounts of pain and that I hated everything in the entire world, especially because I was no longer comforted by my tribe. I went into a hole in my own world, where no one could find me. I prayed that the world would gobble me up. Why had they all died, and I survived? Dying would have been easier than having to deal with the pain of the situation, and the pain in my body and soul.

I wanted to die.

I couldn't change anything; I couldn't fix anything. All I could do was go home.

The airhostess offered us a glass of champagne, which I chugged down in one gulp, anything to help take the edge of the pain away. Taking my seat, I tried to get as comfortable as I could, knowing the next twenty-four hours would be hell. The air was stuffy; my shallow breaths just made it feel even more stifled. I put my earphones on and listened to some classical music, hoping that I would sleep through the majority of the trip; make it all go away again.

* * *

Day six after the accident.

Home.

Twenty-four hours on a plane, one stop over, and I was still in the same amount of pain, if not more. Familiar blue waters shimmered below as the plane descended. Yes, I was home. A surge of feelings went through me. I didn't want to be back on Australian soil, not without my friends.

A hand reached down to me. It was an Australian security intelligence officer assisting me as I tried to move out of my chair. I cried out in pain. Moving from the aircraft to the passenger walkway, the air of Australia filled my nostrils like a fresh burst of sunshine. And while it would have normally made me feel uplifted, the scent only increased my mixed emotions even more. Doors were opened for us, leading us through secret tunnels I didn't even know existed. It was the type of thing you would only ever see in a Hollywood movie.

Hobbling down the alleyway, I wondered how much further it was, and if I could make it. There was no wheelchair waiting for me this time, and I had no one to hold me up physically, or emotionally. The carpet was scratchy underneath my bare, aching feet. Pain shot up my legs with every step. I was desperate to stop moving.

A foreign affairs officer suddenly pushed open what looked like a wall panel, and instantly there they were, my family.

Silent tears streamed down my face and then, they stopped abruptly.

I was home.

I didn't want to be home.

I hated being home.

I wanted to be anywhere but home; I just wanted to be with my friends. They knew how I felt. No one at home could understand.

My body stiffened. All my fellow passengers ran towards their families, embracing them in what was the love they had been longing for, but I just stood there like a statue, unable to move forward, unable to breathe. I wanted the floor to open up and take me.

Mum was crying.

Dad raced over to me, calling out in the way that only Dad could, 'Tiffy!'

I started to soften.

He must have been able to sense that I was unsettled as he threw his enormous arms around me, hugging me.

I yelled out in pain.

'Sorry, possum,' he said, looking at me with concern in his eyes. 'It'll be alright,' he whispered in my ear, like a secret being shared when I was a little girl.

'Oh my darling girl!' Mum said through sobs, as she too embraced me, and again I yelled out in pain. 'Sorry, darling, I'm just so glad to see you. I thought you were dead.'

'But Mum, I called you, I told you I was alive,' I said to her in a voice of utter frustration – they just didn't get it. I didn't get it.

'I know, I know, darling, but I just couldn't believe it until I saw you.'

She looked down at my bare, swollen, black feet. Horror struck her eyes. She hadn't seen the rest of my body yet, for now it appeared the same, covered in clothes, but underneath it was much worse with cuts and bruises covering almost every inch of my body.

Matthew came over and hugged me gently. 'Looks like I should have been taking care of you, not Mum and Dad,' he said winking.

I gave him a tiny smile and ruffled his hair.

Another secret door, another secret passageway, led my family and I out into the sunlight I smelt only moments before, and still, the feelings of unease hadn't dissipated. A foreign affairs officer, the same one who reached down to help me out of the plane, started speaking into his earpiece, informing his commander that he had the package and was heading out.

Dad nudged me in the arm. *Thank God he missed my ribs!* 'This is so cool, Tiffy, just like the movies.'

I smiled, looking up at him. Nothing had changed in him; he was still my rock and safety net. I grabbed his hand and held on for dear life.

✳ ✳ ✳

Day nine after the accident.

I did nothing but continually sleep for what felt like the rest of my life. I never left my bedroom, never left the house, and never went down to my special place. Only slept. It was the only way I could deal with anything. I refused to talk to anyone. I couldn't bring myself to cry, feeling too selfish. In my mind, my pain wasn't nearly as painful as what those families that had lost someone would be experiencing. People called, came by the house, sent cards and flowers. I flatly refused to speak to anyone, even Mum and Dad.

I started to wither away.

I watched the television in silence, as the Ecumenical Service in

Switzerland was held for the bereaved families of all my friends, holding onto my own hands and squeezing them tightly, almost cutting off my circulation. I watched on, seeing the water flowing, now clear and peaceful. A sprig of wattle was thrown into the Saxeten Brook as a remembrance for each individual Australian who had passed. I listened to the Governor General Sir William Deane making his speech – 'It is still winter at home'.

I was still unable to cry.

I looked out to our farm, the wattle now in bloom. I stared at it for as long as my eyes would remain open. I sat there in silence, my chest hurt like what I imagine a heart attack to feel like, while saliva filled my mouth, and my body shook and shivered with sweat, but still, I sat there staring – full of everything and full of nothing.

Flashbacks along with the nightmares came to me at every stage of sleep. These nightmares were filled with water and brutal men, strangulation as water spurted out of my mouth, legs throwing themselves around my body like a circus acrobat. I would wake up, every time I slept, screaming in a lather of sweat and unable to breathe with the blankets thrown around the room. Mum and Dad would be sitting by my bedside, trying to help in every possible way they could. The accident was starting to have its way with me – taking over my life, continuing to take my breath away until maybe I had none left.

✳ ✳ ✳

Day thirteen after the accident.

After another night of torment, I awoke to find a hot cup of tea by my bed, and Mum smiling at me.

'Come and have some breakfast with us,' she suggested.

I gingerly got out of bed, making my way ever so slowly to the family room with my teacup.

The television was on. I stared out the window at the wattle in the paddock. My ears then zeroed in on the announcement coming from newsreader's lips.

'There will be an Ecumenical Service of remembrance today for the fourteen young people from Australia who died in the canyoning tragedy in Switzerland. It will be held at St Christopher's Cathedral, in the Canberra suburb of Manuka, on Monday 9 August at noon. Representatives of both parties of the Australian Government will be in attendance along with representatives of the Diplomatic Corps. A warm invitation is extended to all members of the public who would like to attend.'

'Mum, what time is it?' I called out – panic filled my voice, my heart was beating so fast, adrenaline was surging through my body.

'7.30, why?' Mum called out to me.

'What are you doing today?' I asked, praying that she had nothing on.

'Oh, some office work and meeting up with—'

I cut her off mid sentence; it was the most I had spoken since I arrived home, 'Mum, can you cancel it? I need to go to Canberra,' I called back.

Mum entered the family room where I was seated and glued to the television, pointing at the screen, tears filling my eyes.

Mum looked at the screen, then back at me. 'Vic!' she called down the hallway. 'Tiff and I are going to Canberra. I need you to help us get ready.' Mum rubbed my back, leaning into me. 'Come on, I'll help you get ready.'

It was the fastest I'd moved since the accident. Quickly showering and getting dressed, Mum and I made our way to Canberra in just less than four hours, and in time for the service.

Entering the cathedral, I shied away from any cameras. The media had surrounded the building, bringing instant flashbacks of being in the chalet.

We stood in a long line, queuing at the door, with an array of people dressed in suits and uniforms. One by one, everyone had to sign in, providing their name and an explanation of why they were there.

Once we reached the front of the queue, I stared at the black record book and then at the lady standing behind the book and protecting the door into the cathedral. She looked like she was in the same uniform as the federal police agents that collected us off the plane.

I couldn't work out what to say.

Leaning onto the table and holding Mum's arm, I looked at the book again. I was now holding up the line.

Mum signed the book, stopped, and then looked at me. 'It's okay,' she said, 'you can tell them who you are, darling. It will be alright.'

The federal police agent on the door looked at me again, but this time with a different look on her face. Mum handed me the pen.

My hands started shaking, my heart began to race, and pounding started in my throat and ears. I wrote down my name and looked at the lady on the door.

'Why are you here?' asked the lady, looking at me with a confused expression on her face.

Saying nothing, I looked at her tentatively, then back down at the black registration book. I wrote 'Survivor'.

The lady gasped reading my word. She spoke into her headpiece and immediately more agents came over to me, ushering Mum and I to a discrete area of the cathedral with fewer seats. I was so relieved to be safe from the pack of media predators that prowled around the outside of the cathedral.

I stared at the stained-glass windows and the blond brickwork of such a young cathedral. It was nothing like all the cathedrals I had seen in Europe. My heart beat even faster as more flashbacks came to mind.

I stopped looking at the building, blocking out the memories of my trip. My leg began to throb; pain shot through me like electric shocks. I hadn't moved or walked this much in two weeks.

I tried to listen, but all I could hear was the water.

A federal police agent came to us at the end of the service and asked if we would be happy to meet some government officials.

I looked bewildered. 'Why?' I asked.

'They want to meet you,' the office responded.

'Okay,' I replied, trying to make sense of why they would want to meet me. I hobbled over to a group of men in suits, and introductions where made as I shook hands. I looked over to my left and saw Prime Minister, John Howard, only metres away from me – his entourage whisked him away before I could say anything. My attention was turned back to meeting dignitaries.

'Tiffany, please let me introduce to you the opposition leader, Kim Beasley,' announced the federal agent.

Why do they want to meet me? They don't understand; they don't know. No one knows. I thought, as I went through the motions, until I asked Mum if we could please go home.

My body hurt from all the smiling, my heart hurt from all the questions, I was glad to be back in the car and heading back home.

Still, I didn't cry.

Still, I didn't talk.

✳ ✳ ✳

Day seventeen after the accident.

My body was getting worse and worse by the day, as was my mindset. I was breaking down, in all forms. My parents were anxious about me. Mum insisted that I go to the doctors in Australia, as she wasn't so convinced that my injuries were only bruising. She had been trying over the course of the weeks to get me to go, but I wouldn't. I wouldn't do anything. I would make every excuse under the sun until finally, I couldn't think of any other reason not to go.

It had been many years since I had had my mother with me in the doctor's consulting room. I felt suffocated. But she gave me no choice; she needed to know what was going on. I too didn't know what was going on or how to handle any of the things that I was thinking or feeling. I'd started not to care. However, it looked like I was going to have to start talking. The doctor sitting opposite me gave me no choice either.

I blew my nose in the surgery as the consultation started. I felt like I was under the water again, with only babbling noise around me. The doctor and Mum were talking, but I couldn't hear what they were saying. More mud came out of my nose.

It was still there, inside me.

I showed the doctor. She looked on in horror, as did Mum; I hadn't told or shown anyone the mud still coming out of my body. It was all stuck in my cuts – in particular, my wrist, though it was starting to heal. I could see it buried underneath the skin, a piece of Switzerland.

I left it there.

Finally, someone started to take some notice of my pain levels and began to understand what I was going through physically. X-rays and blood tests were done, and a referral was given to see a psychologist, and some pain relief was prescribed. Thank God, I was finally given some pain relief.

The extent of my injuries came into full light after my medical tests. I had four broken ribs, with particles of rib floating around my chest. My left tibia was fractured, split in half from the ankle almost to my knee. I had a dislocated jaw, and soft-tissue damage to both of my legs, but by now it was too late to have a cast put on my leg. There was also nothing they could do for my ribs, jaw or soft-tissue damage. It appeared that the first round of X-rays were taken so soon after the incident that they didn't show up any calcifications on any of my injuries.

Soon after the extent of my injuries was revealed, I began having sweet cravings and excessive thirst. I thought I was emotional eating, but with all the apricot nectar and sugary foods I was consuming, I started losing weight rapidly. I couldn't work out why I was loosing weight given how much sugar I was consuming. I felt like my mind was playing tricks on me until I almost ended up in a diabetic coma.

Eventually, I was diagnosed with insulin-dependant diabetes, a condition I have to manage for the rest of my life. The ramming of the log into my torso had damaged my pancreas, along with the intense stress my body had experienced, my pancreas had now given up on me. At times, I wished I had given up on me too, but I couldn't. It wasn't what I was sent to earth to do. I knew that now.

Relief started to sink into my body with the right medication. But this was only the physical pain. My mental anguish slowly etched its way into life, as flashbacks and nightmares continued on a daily basis for months on end. I was suffering from Post Traumatic Stress Disorder.

* * *

Day twenty after the accident.

Mum made a phone call to a girl I had mentioned to her. The only one I talked about, if or when I talked. A girl whom she had never met, but she knew that this girl could help us – Cassandra.

'Hi, is this Cassandra?' Mum said.

'Yes,' Cassandra replied.

'This is Tiff's mum. I wondered if I could have a chat with you.'

'Of course, how is Tiff?' Cassandra asked.

'She's not doing so good,' Mum replied, crying into the phone. 'I wouldn't normally do this, but I was wondering, now that you're back home, do you think it would be possible at all for you to visit? You're the only one she talks about. I can't get her out of bed. I'm so worried about her, please, do you think you could help?'

'I'll be on the next plane,' Cassandra replied.

Driving to the airport that afternoon to pick Cassandra up, I was absorbed in my own whirlpool of mixed emotions – anger at having to be home still dominated. I noticed how familiar the country was as we travelled down the motorway. The familiarity made my chest ache with the thought that I didn't want to be there. I still should have been overseas exploring. I also felt nervous about seeing Cassandra. What would happen when I saw her? Would I feel relief? Joy? Heartache?

I was in less pain, thanks to the pain relief, and also because I knew that I would soon have someone who understood what I was feeling, without me having to talk about it again.

Cassandra walked out of the airport gate, backpack on and with her familiar kind eyes shining brightly on me. She raced up towards me as I hobbled over to her.

My heart skipped a beat when I reached out to her, relief washing over me. We embraced like we hadn't seen each other in what felt like an eternity. And finally, I sobbed on her shoulder and her on mine. My kindred spirit had come to save me again.

＊ *＊* *＊*

Back on the farm, with a thermos nestled into the dry blades of grass and cups of hot tea in our hands, I shared my special place with Cassandra. I could finally go back there again. Back to enjoy my sacred place in the world, back to being able to open up and reflect on the memories of my recent past.

Slowly, we began to talk, sitting side by side, looking out into the paddock of calm, with the magpies warbling and bellbirds singing their sweet song, filling the space with peace. And I began to open up, letting all of my emotions start to free themselves as they seeped out of my raw wounds, listening to my intuition and accepting myself once more, knowing Cassandra really listened and understood me. The serenity from my special place was starting to sink back into me and also into Cassandra. All the turmoil, the anguish, the anger, and the hatred all began to subside.

Flickers of sunlight shone through the eucalyptus and onto my chest, as I bared my soul, filling it with hope and light instead of darkness and death. I knew now that I could do it. I could make it on my own. Broken, but whole.

I am Brave Enough Now.

Epilogue

OLDER NOW – WISER? PERHAPS?

On my adventures, I found that an essential part of understanding how to see yourself in the world and what to take from it, are memories of childhood – memories of moments that make us grow, moulding us and teaching us so much. The influence of others; our family, relationships, friends, strangers; our experiences all come together like a soup of inspiration for us to live the life that we are destined to live, and to walk to the path that has been mapped out just for us. Even with the odds stacked up against you, you can become, do, see and be anything. When this happens, magic comes your way and you not only feel awakened within yourself, but it also spreads like wildfire for others to join in.

I have now come to understand that with every day being new, you can be whatever it is you want to be or don't want to be. You have the opportunity to be an illusionist in your own life, hiding behind a facade of magic tricks, staring into glass mirrors while reflecting on what your life currently is, or what your life was, or what you want your life to be. Life is standing there in front of you, as you, within you – with the alchemy of the universe driving us to stay on our path and complete the journey.

I'm older than my friends were when they left this earth. I found my way through the difficult years of grief and pain; studied hard (again), and changed my career (multiple times); found my divine, wonderful, loving, supporting husband. And I now have children of my own, and as a parent myself, I look back on this chapter of my life and acknowledge all the many mistakes that I made, and there were many.

If I had listened better to myself and what was best for me, I would never have kept secrets from my family. I would have shared my pain from the relationship with Patrick and allowed my family to help me remove myself from it. I would have opened up to them and allowed myself to be vulnerable, so that I could overcome my fear and shame, with their help. They have never judged me nor condemned me for any part of my life, only supported me in every way they have known how. And I will be forever eternally grateful for all they have ever done for me.

I would not have behaved like I did so many times, but that is the beauty of reflection. We can see who we were, we can see what went wrong, and we can see forward and see change, just like that moment in the canyon when I chose to let go and miraculously survived. It was a moment I have kept within myself many times since, to help me make decisions when I'm not sure which way to turn.

In those moments, I listen, and I trust in the universe so that I may continue on the path I have been destined to take.

My injuries finally healed, though not without lifelong management. My diabetes is a part of who I am today. Time spent in intense therapy at Westmead Hospital, in the Post Traumatic Stress Disorder unit, enabled me to get back into life, a real life, through all the struggles and flippancy that this disorder can bring. I still use some of the many tools that they gave me. And for that I am so incredibly grateful.

My life is filled with so many gifts, all of which have their rollercoaster moments, though had it not been for all of the rollercoaster moments of life, perhaps I wouldn't be who I am today – a strong, confident, compassionate and courageous woman, but then again maybe I always was.

It was the shame I felt that led me into a soulless existence during those years with Patrick, leading to self-destructive behaviours. As Brene Brown, a social researcher, explains: *shame is correlated with addiction, depression, violence, aggression, bulling, suicide and eating disorder. Shame drives two main points, 'not good enough' and 'who do you think you are?'*

Both of which consumed me as I worked my way out of the darkness I had found myself in.

Through my healing and rehabilitation from the accident, I looked inward and began painting again – one of those paintings is hanging in my house. I have looked at it every day of my life ever since. The beauty of the canyon illuminates green off the paper as I witnessed it that day, sitting on the edge with the blue wall of water coming down the mountainside, hitting everyone with a spray of red, with all those lives lost, and the yellow, orange and gold represents their souls going to heaven. It has reminded me to live without hesitation, and to make the most out of every day and enjoy all the moments – the hard, the good, the beautiful.

That's what life is – beautiful, through all its dark and light.

My friends and family are treasured, and I hold them all close to my heart at all times. I have lived a full and wondrous life, a normal life, and an ordinary life. A life that I have worked hard at to make fabulous through listening to others, taking on board their concerns and making the changes necessary to live my truth with love and appreciation of all things, including life itself.

I have never once forgotten my friends from that journey, nor will I ever. That journey shaped me in ways I could never have foreseen. For years after, all I ever wanted to do was to live life to the fullest, to continue on my path living the biggest and the best way that I could. Doing it for myself, but also doing it for those that were lost.

Now I have come to know that I no longer need to live my life as if I am living it for those who died. I need to live it just for myself, for all of me, for all the broken parts of me, for all the fixed parts of me, for the me that I am – the me that is whole.

A me that I found while finding my way through winding roads with all of them leading home.

FACTS ON THE SAXETENBACH GORGE DISASTER

On 27 July 1999, forty-five young people on two separate Contiki tours participated in the activity of canyoning organised by the company Adventure World in the Saxetenbach Gorge, Switzerland. Canyoning is the activity of sliding, floating, swimming and climbing through an area, often a riverine or gorge.

Participants were separated into four groups. Each group entered the canyon at the same point, but started at different times to avoid too many participants being in the same spot at one time.

During the expedition, a flash flood raced down the gorge. A natural dam had formed at the top of the mountain, but a thunderstorm caused the dam wall to break, flooding the canyon, taking everything in its path.

The first group to enter into the canyon included twelve participants. Ten of whom were on the banks at the time the flood reached them.

All survived.

The second group to enter the canyon, with eleven participants – including Tiffany – were in the gorge between large boulders when the wall of water hit.

Only three survived.

The third group, consisting of eleven participants, was directly behind Tiffany's group, and situated where the absailing was and where the second group had just been. They too, were stuck in the middle of the gorge.

Only one survived.

The fourth and final group of eleven participants never entered the canyon.

Twenty-one people died that day.

People from Australia, New Zealand, South Africa, England and Switzerland died. Eighteen were tourists, of that fourteen were Australian, and three were canyon guides.

At the time, it was the largest number of deaths of young Australians outside of Australia at one time during times of peace.

The flood hit at 6 pm. By 7 pm the media had been alerted of the incident and the news rapidly spread across the globe.

Some of the bodies washed up in the Lake Brienz at the bottom of the canyon. One body has never been recovered.

Identifying the dead bodies was a severe problem for the Swiss authorities. Language barriers, time zones, lack of local records of individuals or family members of the deceased all contributed to the difficulty. Due to the number of bodies, eight travel companions opted to help pre-identify the dead to help assist the authorities, this ensured that families were connected to the right body. The bodies were badly traumatised, some had to be identified through DNA and dental analysis. Tattoos assisted where there was no other way to identify the body due to trauma.

On 5 August 1999, Sir William Deane, governor general of Australia, flew to Interlaken for an Ecumenical Service for the victims of the canyoning tragedy, held at the Saxetenbach Gorge with families of the victims. A memorial rock was unveiled with the victims' names on a plaque and a tribute wall where wreaths, letters and flowers were left for the deceased. The governor general's speech at that service has since been recognised as one of Australia's most important speeches for international relations and has been used as part of the New South Wales Year Twelve English curriculum.

Adventure World went out of business. Six company directors were charged and found guilty of manslaughter through culpable negligence. They were given suspended jail sentences of between two and five months and fined between 4000 and 7500 Swiss francs.

Response units around the world have since changed the way that they manage natural-disaster rescues and trauma treatment for survivors, including integrating mental health care plans now as part of the recovery from the learnings during this disaster.

'IT IS STILL WINTER AT HOME'

We are gathered in great sadness to mourn the deaths of the twenty-one young people who were killed in the canyoning accident near here, last week. They came from five nations – Switzerland, the United Kingdom, South Africa, New Zealand and Australia. Their loss is a profound tragedy for their families and friends who are in the thoughts and the prayers of all of us at this service today. We pray with them for their loved ones who have died. And we also pray that, in the words of our Lord (Matthew 5:4), they will truly be comforted.

Fourteen of the victims of the tragedy came from Australia. Collectively, their deaths represent probably the greatest single peacetime loss of young Australians outside our own country. That loss affects not only their families and friends, dreadful though that is. It also deeply affects our nation as a whole and all of its people.

I have, as governor-general of Australia, with Senator John Herron of our government, come here on behalf of Australia and of all Australians, to mourn them, to be with and to sympathise with their family members and friends who are here and to demonstrate how important they were to their homeland. For us, the tragedy is somehow made worse by the fact that they died so far away from the homes, the families, the friends and the land they loved so well.

Australia and Switzerland are on opposite sides of the globe. Yet, in this age of modern telecommunications, one effect of the disaster has been to bring our two countries closer together. On every night since the accident, Switzerland has been in every Australian home that has been tuned into the television news, as well as on the radio, in all our newspapers and other media outlets. Conversely, the fact that two-thirds of those who died came from Australia has given rise to an increased awareness here in Switzerland of my country and its people.

Switzerland has, of course, itself experienced the shock and sorrow of overseas tragedy in the past. Perhaps that has heightened the sympathy and understanding which it has shown in recent days. I have already had the privilege of meeting with you, Madam President and with Vice-President Ogi and exchanging condolences. I would, on this solemn occasion, like to express to the Swiss authorities and to the people of Switzerland, particularly the people of the Wilderswil and Interlaken regions, our abiding gratitude for all the help and assistance they have provided in the aftermath of the tragedy. In particular, I pay tribute to the bravery of all those who worked in the rescue efforts. We thank them for their skill and dedication.

I also particularly mention the competence, the compassion and the kindness of all who have helped to look after the survivors and the relatives who have come here.

The young people – certainly the young Australians – who have been killed all shared the spirit of adventure, the joy of living, the exuberance and the delight of youth. That spirit inspired their lives and lit the lives of all who knew them, until the end. We remember that and so many other wonderful things about them as we mourn them and grieve for young lives cut so tragically short. And all of us feel and share in their collective loss. For these twenty-one young men and women were part – a shining part – of our humanity. As John Donne wrote, 'No man is an island'. Anyone's 'death diminishes' us all because we are all 'involved in mankind'.

Yesterday, my wife and I, together with family members and friends of the Australian victims, visited the canyon where the accident occurred. There, in memory of each of the fourteen young people who came from our homeland, we cast into the Saxetenbach fourteen sprigs of wattle, our national floral emblem, which we had brought with us from Government House in Canberra. Somehow, we felt that was bringing a little of Australia to them.

It was also, in a symbolic way, helping to bring them home to our country. That is not to suggest that their spirit and their memory will not linger forever, here in Switzerland, at the place where they died. Rather, it is to suggest that a little part of Switzerland has become and will always be, to some extent, part of Australia. As it will also be part of the other countries outside Switzerland – New Zealand, South Africa and the United Kingdom – from whence they came.

It is still winter at home. But the golden wattles are coming into bloom. Just as these young men and women were in the flower of their youth. And when we are back in Australia, we will remember how the flowers and the perfume and the pollen of their and our homeland were carried down the river where they died to Lake Brienz in this beautiful country on the far side of the world.

May they all rest with God.

ACKNOWLEDGEMENTS

Twenty years ago, I started writing this book. All too raw, too hard and too emotional, I shut down the bulky, clunky computer and closed the door. But the little niggle within me never went away. I knew the story was there, and it was one that needed to be told. Now, after the past two years of writing this book, I am so incredibly humbled and overwhelmed by the amount of love and dedication that has helped me develop this book. Without your support, it would not be what it is today and nor would I.

I have created new and lasting friendships, and evolved as a person and a writer throughout this process, and for that I will be forever grateful. Thank you doesn't seem enough.

My incredible husband for believing in me – I still have the post-it note you wrote to me and stuck on the mirror in the bathroom the day I completed my first draft. I have looked to that note daily, smiling, even when times were tough. You have taught me so much about myself and the world. Your love never falters, and I am so incredibly thankful for all that you do for me and our family. I would not be where I am today without your love, devotion, support, guidance and belief in me. Thank you. I love you more each and every day.

To my children who have cooked for me when things have been due, brought me cups of tea through power-writing phases and danced in celebration with me all around the house. You are my sunshine, I love you, and I am so proud of you.

To my mum, for listening to me, almost every day for the past two years and the years before that. You support me through everything. You are always, ALWAYS there for me, even when I've been trying. I love you. Thank you.

To my dad for always being my rock.

My brother, you still hold my hand, though somewhat bigger now, when I need you, and I when you need me. Thank you for always making me laugh, for loving me like only a brother can.

And to the rest of my family, thank you for standing by me in times of triumph and in times of tears. Your belief in me has been stronger than the most robust iron chains. Thank you.

Emma – for your love, your tears of joy and your belief in me and our friendship forever more. I will always have my hand in your pocket.

Fordy – how glad I am that I answered the phone and moved into our shared townhouse 19 years ago: a lifetime of laughs and tears. You will always be my big brother.

Lara – for your encouragement, strength, courage and support, for being a confidante when I needed it.

My walking girls, Georgia, Silvia & Robyn – your listening ears have set me on the straight and narrow so many times. I value our special walking tribe. We are unique, and I love you all for it.

Marta, for your kind-heartedness, your honesty and belief in me. A total stranger, now a friend. Thank you.

Katrina Logan. Your enthusiasm, help and belief in me has driven me to the next step many times over.

Emma Hood. The crazy blonde is still as mad as ever and loves you even more.

To my incredible editing team, you have all played such a pivotal role in my writing and in my life. To Rachel, Tricia, Michele and Sam, thank you for helping me make this book what it is today.

Rachel, a cold and blowy moment in the playground turned out to be the spark of a kindred friendship in the making. Thank you for teaching me so much, for supporting me, for working with me through the initial stages. It was because of you that I was able to make this book what it is. Thank you.

Heather, your constant support, encouragement and belief in my truth-telling has filled my soul on many occasions. Thank you.

My writers' group, thank you for sharing your beautiful craft with me and supporting me through this crazy journey of writing. I've learned so much, and I'm privileged to know you all.

Yael Maree, a crazy friend who I couldn't be without. You have taught me so much, stuck with me and walked the path. I am forever grateful. I promise to get you tickets! Thank you.

To Nan, for that very first step to making my purpose a reality. To my launch team, Di, Nicky, Emma, Cassandra, Fordy, Brydie, Dena and Dave. You guys rock, thank you for being by my side through all the ups and downs.

Michele Perry from Wordplay editing, I will never forget the moment I finished reading the comments on the first edit. So overwhelmed with emotion, I cried for 3 hours. To work with you has been nothing short of a pleasure. You have taught me so much, gone over and above in your work with me, and I have loved every minute.

To Ann and Dixie from Indie Experts, you have taken me under your wing and worked with me every step of the way. Thank you for your guidance, support and dedication, your customer service is second to none!

To Bronny, from Little Train, for new adventures to be had!

For my friends whose lives got cut way too short. You will always be with me and with all those who loved you. May you rest in peace.

And for Cassandra. For putting your head up over the seat 20 years ago and never ever looking back. I love you.

NOTES

1. TED 2012, Brené Brown, *Listening to Shame*, viewed 20 June 2018, <https://www.ted.com/talks brene_brown_listening_to_shame#t-867487>.

CPSIA information can be obtained
at www.ICGtesting.com
Printed in the USA
BVHW042001230719
554057BV00054B/563/P

9 780648 587903